This book belongs to

Anna

and

Money

Between Us

A 52-Week Keepsake Devotional for Daughters and Moms

VICKI COURTNEY

B&H
PUBLISHING GROUP

Nashville, Tennessee

Published in association with the literary agency D.C. Jacobson & Associates, LLC, an Author Management Company, www.dcjacobson.com, and Alive Communications, Inc., an Author Management Company, www.alivecommunications.com.

ISBN 978-1-4336-8789-1

Published by B&H Publishing Group
Nashville, Tennessee

Dewey Decimal Classification: 302
MOTHERS AND DAUGHTERS \ DEVOTIONAL LITERATURE \ WOMEN

Printed in Huizhou, Guangdong, China, June 2016

1 2 3 4 5 6   20 19 18 17 16

Introduction

When my daughter was about your age, we used to play a silly little game when we were in the car. Sometimes, when I noticed she was quiet and deep in thought, I would grab a penny out of the change tray in the front console of my car and pass it back to her and say, "Penny for your thoughts." Maybe it had been a rough day because a friend had left her out and her feelings had been hurt. Or maybe she was stressed about the math test the next day and worried she wouldn't have enough time to study after her gymnastics class. Maybe she was frustrated with an annoying boy in her grade who was always picking on her during PE. Or maybe she was just daydreaming and thinking about her weekend plans and wishing it was already Friday. Whatever it was, that penny could usually get her to start talking, even if it took a little more convincing on my part (like a stop at her favorite snow-cone stand on the way home!).

I know the penny game sounds pretty corny, but I want to let you in on a little secret. Moms will try just about anything to get their daughters to open up and talk to them. Even though we're moms and we seem way out of touch with your world, the truth is, we used to be your age. Believe it or not, we faced many of the same challenges and frustrations you do. Even though it was a long, long time ago, we can still remember some of the things that weighed heavy on our hearts and how confused and alone we felt at times. The truth is, we don't want you to feel that way as you walk through your tween years. More importantly, we want to pass along some truths from the Bible that can help guide you through the tough times. And they say a penny won't buy much in today's world.

I'm pretty sure I got more than my money's worth with that silly penny game! We won't always be able to fix your problems, but we can point you to the One who knows you better than anyone. And He doesn't even need a penny to know what's on your heart and mind!

I guess you could say this book is like that penny I used to hand my daughter. I wrote it to get you and your mom talking about some of the challenges you might face as a tween. The book is laid out in fifty-two weeks, and each week has a story and a Bible verse to go along with it. I hand picked many of the same Bible passages my daughter and I talked about when she was your age. I also included some questions to answer (for both you and your mom) and a fun activity and weekly challenge at the end. As you go through each week, I encourage you and your mom to write down your answers so you can look back years from now and have a keepsake of your Between Us moments and memories.

So what are you waiting for? Turn the page, and let's get started!

A penny for your thoughts . . .

Vicki Courtney

Contents

Week 1:   Pretty Packaging .11

Week 2:   Look at the Birds!. 18

Week 3:   Seven Quintillion 25

Week 4:   Not to Brag, But 33

Week 5:   Tear #5,391 41

Week 6:   Quitting the Drama Club 47

Week 7:   Taking Home the Prize. 55

Week 8:   Jealousy Versus Joy 63

Week 9:   One Step at a Time. 71

Week 10: One of a Kind. 78

Week 11: Better Than Gold 86

Week 12: Whatever 93

Week 13: Tough Times. 100

Week 14: Be Happy! 106

Week 15: The Remedy for Worry 113

Week 16: First Things First 121

Week 17: Inside-Out 129

Week 18: Knock, Knock 136

Week 19: Share the Good News! 142

Week 20: Grrrrrrr 149

Week 21: Helping Hands. 157

Week 22: Pinky Swear Promise 165

Week 23: Above All Else. 172

Week 24: A New Pendant 179

Week 25: Clean Slate. 187

Week 26: A Day to Remember. 194

Week 27: Weekend Friends 201

Week 28: Forgive and Forget. 208

Week 29: Loving the Unlovable 214

Week 30: Do-Over. 222

Week 31: Beauty That Lasts. 229

Week 32: Run for the Prize 236

Week 33: The Greatest Gain 244

Week 34: Made by God .252

Week 35: Time for a Workout! 259

Week 36: One Way. 267

Week 37: Heart of the Matter. 275

Week 38: A New, Improved You. 282

Week 39: Are You a Peacemaker? 290

Week 40: Don't Miss Out. 298

Week 41: Rooted in God's Love 306

Week 42: More Than Enough. 314

Week 43: God Is Good. 322

Week 44: A Way of Escape .329

Week 45: Time to Pray. 337

Week 46: This Little Light of Mine 344

Week 47: If You're Happy and You Know It 352

Week 48: No Greater Love. .359

Week 49: Say It Like You Mean It 366

Week 50: More Fruit, Please 374

Week 51: Do You Have a Reservation? 382

Week 52: Who Do You Say I Am? 390

Week 1:
Pretty Packaging

Bible Reading

But the LORD said to Samuel, "Do not look at his appearance or his stature, because I have rejected him. Man does not see what the LORD sees, for man sees what is visible, but the LORD sees the heart."
—1 Samuel 16:7

Read the passage aloud and listen carefully for the answers to the following questions:

What does man see?

_____

What does the Lord see?

_____

Bringing It Home

Kate stared at the pile of presents in the middle of the floor. She looked forward to the family gift exchange each year at Christmastime. The instructions were simple: Each child in the family was to bring a wrapped gift costing no more than five dollars. You could bring something fun and useful, or you could bring a joke gift. Last year, Kate hit the jackpot and scored a giant bag of Sour Patch Kids. She was happy to share some with the other kids—after, of course, she picked out all the orange ones since they were her favorite. Her brother hadn't been so lucky when it came time to pick his gift. He'd ended up with a pair of his cousin Dillon's smelly gym socks!

It was Kate's turn to pick a gift. She had her eye on a gift that was wrapped neatly in silver paper. It had a beautiful red and white ribbon attached to the top. It was the prettiest present in the pile, and Kate was sure it contained something good on the inside. Her cousin Lindsey warned her that it might be a joke gift. "No way!" said Kate. "This is the one I want." As she plucked it from the pile, she couldn't wait to see what was inside. She slowly unwrapped the gift, sliding the pretty ribbon off the top. She tore the paper at the end and slid the box out carefully. As she lifted the lid of the box, one of her cousins taunted her, "It's going to be a dud!"

Unfortunately, her cousin was right. Her heart sank as she pulled back the tissue wrap inside the box to reveal . . . her cousin Dillon's smelly gym socks! Her brother had kept the socks and wrapped them up for this year's gift exchange. Seriously?! Kate was disappointed, but she knew this was part of the game. You win some and you lose some. Kate learned a valuable lesson that day at the gift exchange: What you see is not always what you get. Kate chose the gift because of the pretty packaging and assumed it would be the best gift.

What does God's Word say?

God gave His prophet Samuel the task of choosing the next king of Israel. (A prophet is someone God chose to be His "mouthpiece," or someone who would let the people know what He was thinking.) He told Samuel, "I am sending you to Jesse of Bethlehem because I have selected a king from his sons" (1 Samuel 16:1). Samuel immediately thought the next king would be Eliab, who was the oldest of Jesse's eight sons. He seemed like the logical choice for the future king. In fact, when Samuel saw Eliab, he said, "Certainly the LORD's anointed one is here before Him" (v. 6). "Anointed" means "chosen." But the Lord didn't choose Eliab as the next king.

One by one, Jesse's sons passed by the prophet Samuel, and after he had met seven of the sons, he declared, "The Lord has not chosen these." But there was one brother missing in the lineup that day. The youngest brother, David, was out in the pastures tending the sheep. At the Lord's prompting, Samuel asked Jesse to send for his youngest son.

And yep, you guessed it: David was the one God chose to be the next king. While man is drawn to outward appearance, God is drawn to the heart. God chose David because He saw something beautiful in David's heart and He knew he would be the best king to lead the people.

As you get older, you will see many examples of people judging one another based on appearance. You will even meet girls who may be pretty on the outside, but not so much on the inside. This is why it's important to remember what is most important to God: a beautiful heart.

Think About It

What's more important to you: being pretty on the outside or pretty on the inside?

Talk About It

Questions to ask your mom:

When you were my age, did you care more about being beautiful on the outside or beautiful on the inside?

Can you remember doing something and being complimented for your beautiful heart? What was it?

Questions for your mom to ask you:

What makes someone beautiful on the inside?

Which compliment would you rather receive: "You are pretty" or "You have a beautiful heart"? Why?

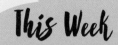

This Week

Be on the lookout for something your mom does that God would consider "beautiful on the inside." Have your mom do the same thing. Ask her to tell you when she notices you doing something that is "beautiful on the inside." Before you read your devo for next week, share what you noticed.

My mom is beautiful because:

_____

_____

_____

_____

My daughter is beautiful because:

_____

_____

_____

_____

Keep Going

Look up 1 Peter 3:3–4.

In the picture below, write down qualities of a beautiful heart. (Hint: Look at verse 4.) Can you think of others? Write them down also.

Week 2:
Look at the Birds!

Bible Reading

"This is why I tell you: Don't worry about your life, what you will eat or what you will drink; or about your body, what you will wear. Isn't life more than food and the body more than clothing? Look at the birds of the sky: They don't sow or reap or gather into barns, yet your heavenly Father feeds them. Aren't you worth more than they?"
—Matthew 6:25–26

Read the passage aloud and listen carefully for the answers to the following questions:

God tells us not to worry about what?

_____

_____

What are we told to look at as an example of how God takes care of us and meets our needs?

_____

_____

Bringing It Home

Tessa could tell something was wrong by the worried look on her mother's face. Her father had called a family meeting after dinner, and the last time that had happened, it was bad news. Her grandfather had unexpectedly passed away. Tessa's stomach was in knots thinking about what the announcement could possibly be. Finally, her dad began to speak. "Kids, your mother and I didn't want to worry you with this, but I lost my job a couple of weeks ago." Tessa breathed a sigh of relief that it wasn't as bad as the news last time. However, she could tell it was very serious. Her dad continued, "I wanted to be honest with you about this because there is a possibility I may have to take a job in another town, which means we would have to move."

Tessa couldn't breathe. She had lived in the same house, on the same street, in the same town since she was a baby. Her friends at school and church had been her friends since her preschool and kindergarten days. She had always felt bad for the new kids who came into her school; and now, she might be one of the "new kids." She began to softly cry. She knew her parents were worried and didn't want to move, so it wouldn't be fair to throw a fit. Besides, she had to be a good example for her little brother. He was only in first grade, so he didn't completely understand what all was involved in moving.

Her father went on to share that her mother's job didn't pay enough to take care of all the bills, and they would need to be very careful about the money they spent while her dad was searching for a job. As if moving wasn't enough to worry about, now she had to worry about whether they would have enough money to pay for food. And Christmas was right around the corner. Forget about the tablet she had asked her parents to get her. She felt guilty for having the thought. Did God care about finding her dad a job? Would He take care of them if her dad didn't find a job?

What does God's Word say?

In Philippians 4:19, we are reminded that "God will supply all your needs according to His riches in glory in Christ Jesus." He gave the example of the birds as a reminder of that promise. He knows our needs and He will meet them. Guaranteed. The birds don't gather up their food and hide it (like squirrels!). They don't have a food pantry in their nest stocked up with a week's supply of worms and insects. They are dependent on God to meet their needs day by day, moment by moment, one slimy worm at a time. I'm pretty sure they don't wake up in the morning and panic, "Oh no, what if I don't find food today?" They leave the nest knowing they will find food because God met their needs the

day before. And the day before that. And the day before that. As far back as they can remember, God has met their needs. And yet, God reminds us that we are more important to Him than the birds.

For most of us, our closets are filled with clothes, our stomachs are filled with food, and our homes are filled with love. Every day. And every day before that. It's always been that way, for as long as we can remember. For that reason, it's sometimes easy to forget that God has been faithful to meet our needs. We don't worry so much about what we will eat, what we will drink, or what we will wear. However, we do worry about other things. "Will I get the teacher I want next year?" "Will I make friends at my new school?" "Will I get a cell phone someday like my friends?" "Will my dad find a job?" "Will my grandmother get well?"

You may have worries, but God promises to meet your needs one day at a time, just like He does for the birds. He may not do it in the way you expect, but He promises to take care of you.

Think About It

Is it hard for you to trust God
to meet your needs?

Talk About It

Questions to ask your mom:

Can you think of a time when you wondered if God would meet your needs? What happened?

_____

_____

_____

_____

Did God take care of you? How?

_____

_____

_____

_____

_____

Questions for your mom to ask you:

Do you ever worry about your life? If so, what kind of things do you worry about?

_____

_____

_____

Has God met your needs before and proven He cares for you?

_____

_____

_____

What are some needs God has met in your life? List as many that come to mind below. (You should be able to come up with a bunch!)

_____

_____

_____

This Week

Be on the lookout for birds. When you see them, take a minute to observe them and then thank God for the reminder that He loves you and is faithful to meet your needs.

Keep Going

God wants us to remember this important truth every time we see birds. Unscramble the words to find the answer!

__ __ __ __ __   __ __ __   __ __ __ __   __ __ __ __

u s t r t   o d G   o t   t e m e   u y r o

__ __ __ __ __   __ __ __   __ __ __   __ __ __ __ .

e s e d n   e o n   y d a   t a   a e m t i .

ANSWER: Trust God to meet your needs one day at a time.

24

Week 3:
Seven Quintillion

Bible Reading

God, how difficult
Your thoughts are for me
to comprehend;
how vast their sum is!
If I counted them,
they would outnumber
the grains of sand.
—Psalm 139:17–18

Read the Bible passage aloud and listen carefully for the answers to the following questions:

Does God think about you?

How often does God think about you?

Bringing It Home

Abbi had looked forward to the sleepover all week, until, that is, the big fight. After pizza, they were going to watch a movie—and that's when the war began. Everyone was naming off movies they wanted to see, but when Abbi suggested one of her favorites, one of the girls burst out laughing. "My sister loves that movie and she's like, five years old, Abbi. Seriously, no one wants to watch that." Abbi felt her face turn red, and she pretended like it didn't bother her. But it did.

It seemed like no matter what her opinion was, Natalie found a way to make fun of it. Last week, Abbi had said she was going shopping after school and when Natalie asked where she was going, she proceeded to make fun of that too. "Ew. I never go in that store anymore. The clothes are so cheap and they fall apart after a few weeks." The week before that, it was about what was in her lunch. "You still eat Fruit Roll-Ups? That's funny." Nothing ever met Natalie's approval. At least nothing Abbi did. Natalie never seemed to make fun of any of the other girls.

What does God's Word say?

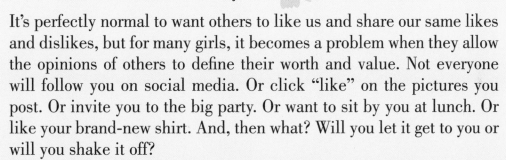

It's perfectly normal to want others to like us and share our same likes and dislikes, but for many girls, it becomes a problem when they allow the opinions of others to define their worth and value. Not everyone will follow you on social media. Or click "like" on the pictures you post. Or invite you to the big party. Or want to sit by you at lunch. Or like your brand-new shirt. And, then what? Will you let it get to you or will you shake it off?

Psalm 139 reminds us that God's thoughts about us outnumber the grains of sand. Have you ever been to the beach before? Do you think it would even be possible to count the grains of sand on the one beach you visited? Or even in your sand bucket? No way!

A science writer, David Blatner, attempted to calculate the number of grains of sand that covered the entire world. He calculated the average size of a grain of sand and then estimated how many were in a teaspoon to figure out a rough estimate of how many it would take to fill all the beaches and deserts in the world. His very rough estimate was 7.5×10^{18} grains of sand or seven quintillion, five hundred quadrillion grains. I've never even heard of a "quintillion" before, have you?! This is what it looks like as a number:

7,500,000,000,000,000,000

Look at it this way: If you were to count to one quintillion and you counted one number every second of the day and night, it would take you approximately 316,889,554 years.

But that's only counting to one quintillion. God's thoughts about us are probably more than seven quintillion! That would take about 221,822,687,800 years!

The next time you find yourself worrying about what others think, remember that number—seven quintillion, smile, and know that you are greatly loved by the God of this universe.

Stop and imagine that is how many thoughts God has about you! Why, then, do we care so much about what others think?

Think About It

Do you think girls your age care too much about what others think?

Talk About It

Questions to ask your mom:

When you were my age, did you care too much about what others thought about you? In what ways? (List them below.)

_____

_____

_____

_____

_____

_____

_____

_____

If you could go back and have a talk with your younger self, what would you tell her?

Dear younger self,

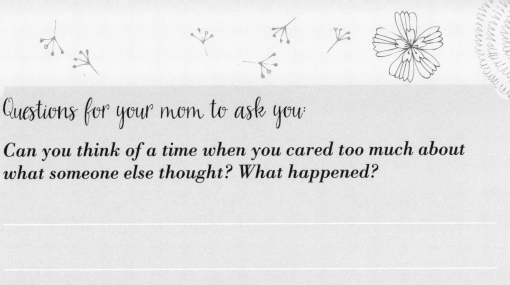

Questions for your mom to ask you:

Can you think of a time when you cared too much about what someone else thought? What happened?

What are some thoughts God might have about you?

This Week

As you go through the week, try to pause when you find yourself caring too much about what someone else thinks of you. Stop and remind yourself of how often God thinks about you.

Keep Going

Both you and your mom write down Psalm 139:17–18 below. Now write the number 7,500,000,000,000,000,000 on a Post-it note or a piece of paper. Put it in your locker, in a school notebook, on your bathroom mirror, or wherever you will see the reminder each day. While you're at it, have your mom do the same thing and tell her to put it somewhere she will see it.

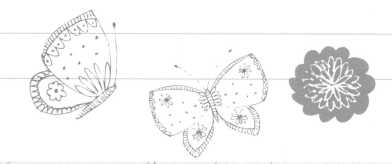

Week 4:
Not to Brag, But...

Bible Reading

Let another praise you,
and not your own mouth—
a stranger, and not
your own lips.
–Proverbs 27:2

Read the Bible passage aloud and listen carefully for the answers to the following questions:

Is it okay to brag on yourself?

_____

Who should you let praise you?

_____

_____

_____

Bringing It Home

I plopped down my lunch tray just in time to hear Addison say those four familiar words she always seemed to say, "Not to brag, but . . ." Of course, what usually followed those four words was a whole lot of bragging about her latest and greatest award, achievement, compliment, or just plain awesomeness. Today was no different. "This past weekend, I won first place at my competitive cheer competition, and my coach said it was my best performance yet." Last week, it had been the A she got on the history exam—the same exam most of the rest of our group had scored a B on. The week before that, it was the awesome summer vacation her family was planning to Disney World. We all knew Addison was talented and smart, and her family had lots of money. We knew these things because she reminded us every day!

Our group of friends had hung out since kindergarten, but we were all starting to get annoyed at her constant bragging. We loved Addison, but we just didn't understand why she felt the need to brag on herself all the time. The more she bragged, the less we wanted to be around her. Lunchtime had turned into the Addison Show, and she made sure we all knew she was the star. Unfortunately, Addison seemed to have no idea that most of us were tired of the same old show and ready to change the channel!

What does God's Word say?

It's a good thing to be confident in yourself and your abilities. However, God's Word tells us not to boast or brag about ourselves. I know this can be hard, especially if you are really excited about something and no one seems to be speaking up. There is nothing wrong with celebrating good news with a few close friends. That is not necessarily bragging. However, if you are pointing to yourself with an attitude that says, "Hey, look at me and how awesome I am," it would be considered bragging. Girls who are in the habit of bragging are fishing for approval from others. It's a warning sign that they base their worth on their successes and failures.

Think About It

Are you a bragger? Or do you usually wait and let others brag on you?

Talk About It

Questions to ask your mom:

Tell me about a time when something awesome happened to you and you remember someone else praising you. How did it feel?

Questions for your mom to ask you:

How do you praise others and celebrate their good news?

_____

_____

_____

_____

Who can you think of right now who could use some praise?

_____

_____

This Week

Read Jeremiah 9:23–24 and underline
what kind of boasting God delights in:

This is what the LORD says:

The wise man must not boast in his wisdom;

the strong man must not boast in his strength;

the wealthy man must not boast in his wealth.

But the one who boasts should boast in this,

that he understands and knows Me—

that I am Yahweh, showing faithful love,

justice, and righteousness on the earth,

for I delight in these things.

When you find yourself
tempted to boast about
something, stop and boast
instead about God.

Keep Going

Take the quiz below to see if you are a bragger.
Put a check mark by your answer.

1. Your teacher just handed back the spelling test from the week
    before. You made a perfect 100 and are super-excited. At
    lunch, you are sitting with some of your classmates and you
    say . . .

___ a. "How did y'all do on the spelling test?" (You know if you
        bring it up, you'll get to tell them what you made!)

___ b. "I got a 100 on the spelling test! What did y'all get?"

___ c. Nothing. You don't want anyone who made a lower grade to
        feel uncomfortable.

2. One of your friends is telling you about her cousin's house and
    how it is huge and has five bedrooms. Your mom and dad were
    talking recently about moving into a bigger house with four or
    five bedrooms. You say . . .

___ a. "Yeah, my parents were talking not long ago about moving
        into a bigger house someday."

___ b. "I'm pretty sure we're moving into a house that big!"

___ c. Nothing. When it's someone else's story, it's rude to try to
        one-up them.

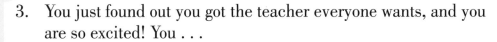

3. You just found out you got the teacher everyone wants, and you are so excited! You . . .

__ a. grab your mom's phone and send a text to a group of your friends and say, "My mom just got the teacher assignments. Who did you get?" (You mainly send the message so you can share who you got as a teacher!)

__ b. grab your mom's phone and send a text to a group of your friends and say, "I got Ms. Leonard! I'm so excited!"

__ c. do nothing. You know there will be many who didn't get the teacher they wanted, and you don't want to rub it in.

If you answered *a* more than once, you are not full-out bragging, but close. Everyone likes to compare results or share good news, but it's best to remain quiet if your good news would make someone else feel bad.

If you answered *b* more than once, you may not mean to be a bragger, but it's probably coming across that way to others. When you have good news you want to share, pause and take a few minutes to think about how your news might affect others and what your motive (reason) really is for sharing it.

If you answered *c* more than once, you are not a bragger. You are sensitive to how your news might make others feel, so you play it safe by saying nothing. If you have good news you want to share, you might share it with a few close friends, but you don't broadcast it to the world.

Week 5:
Tear #5,391

Bible Reading

You keep track of all my sorrows.
You have collected all my tears
in your bottle. You have recorded
each one in your book.
—Psalm 56:8 NLT

Read the passage aloud and listen carefully for the answers to the following questions:

Who keeps track of your sorrows?

_____

_____

What is collected in a bottle?

_____

_____

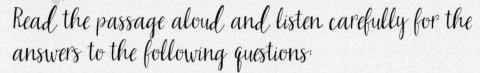

Bringing It Home

Hannah groaned when her alarm went off. Surely, it wasn't morning already. Why was she so tired? And then it hit her. It wasn't a bad dream. The night before, her parents had told her they were getting a divorce. They reassured her that she would be able to spend time with both of them, even though her dad was going to move out of the house and live somewhere else. They told her it wouldn't be the end of the world, but her friend Ellie had divorced parents and was always complaining about having to split her time between two houses and two families. Hannah had cried herself to sleep thinking about how everything was about to change in her family.

Before she fell asleep, she had prayed and asked God to make the problem go away, so her heart would stop hurting. She knew God could do anything, including keeping her family together. And yet, when morning came, the problem was still there. Did God even care about her family? Maybe He was too busy answering bigger prayers about war and cancer and hungry children. She had always believed in God

since the time she was a little girl, and she needed Him now more than ever. Did He even know her heart had been shattered into a billion tiny pieces the night before?

What does God's Word say?

When you experience heartbreak and sadness, God knows about it. In fact, the Bible tells us He knows the reason behind every tear you shed. Isn't that an amazing thought? Unfortunately, no one will escape difficult times, but the good news is that God cares deeply when you are sad or heartbroken. More importantly, you can pour out your heart to Him in prayer and ask Him to comfort you.

Psalm 34:18 reminds us, "The LORD is near the brokenhearted; He saves those crushed in spirit." You cannot shed a single tear without God knowing about it. Even though you can't see God, He is there. He comforts us through the Bible, which is why it's important to read God's Word on a regular basis. Sometimes He comforts us through other people. Other times He comforts us by giving us peace when we pray. God desires that we come to Him first before anyone else.

Think About It

Do you go to God when you are sad or brokenhearted?

43

Talk About It

Questions to ask your mom:

Tell me about a time when you were my age and you were feeling sad about something. What was it? Did you talk to God about it?

_____

_____

_____

_____

Questions for your mom to ask you:

When was the last time you were feeling really sad about something? How does it make you feel to discover that God cares and knows the reason behind each and every tear you shed?

_____

_____

_____

This Week

When you find yourself feeling sad about something, picture God writing down the reason behind your tears. Now, picture Him holding you tight in His arms and comforting you like a loving father would comfort his precious child. Practice going to God first and then sharing your sadness with your mom or dad.

Keep Going

Think of the last few times you felt sad about something. Maybe you even cried. In the space below, write down the reason behind your sadness, much like it describes God doing in Psalm 56:8. Take a minute to thank God for caring about your sadness, even if you didn't realize it at the time.

Week 6:
Quitting the Drama Club

Bible Reading

A dishonest man spreads strife, and a whisperer separates close friends.
—Proverbs 16:28 ESV

Read the passage aloud and listen carefully for the answers to the following questions:

A dishonest man spreads what?

_____

Who separates close friends?

_____

Bringing It Home

Jenna sat down at the lunch table with her friends and noticed the empty seat. "Where's Morgan?" she asked. Kylie and Julia glanced at each other before one of them pointed in the direction of the "cool table." Jenna looked over just in time to hear Morgan's familiar laugh echoing through the lunchroom. Whatever she said must have been entertaining because her new friends were laughing right along with her. This was the third time this month Morgan had told them to save her spot at the lunch table, only to be a no-show. The last time she did it, Jenna asked her later why she didn't sit with them after asking them to save her spot. When Morgan answered, she rambled nervously about how she was planning to sit with their group like always, but one of the girls from the popular table grabbed her arm when she was walking by and dragged her over to the table. You could tell she was totally lying, making it up as she answered.

When Morgan saw Jenna looking at her, she immediately looked away. A few minutes later, she whispered something to one of the girls sitting beside her and they both turned around and looked at their table. Jenna and her friends didn't really have a problem with Morgan sitting somewhere else, but they wished she would just tell them the truth. It wasn't against the law for her to have other friends, but they were tired of her drama. The not showing up, making up excuses, and now, the awkward whispering. Maybe it was time to take a break from Morgan.

What does God's Word say?

Dishonest friends cause strife (drama!), and whisperers can break up friendships. If you look up the word *strife* in the dictionary, you will find that it means "quarrel" or "competition or rivalry." If you substitute that meaning in the verse, it makes it easier to understand:

"A dishonest man spreads strife [quarrels, competition, or rivalry], and a whisperer [gossip] separates close friends."

When you are experiencing drama with your friends, try to be a peacemaker. A peacemaker is someone who does not go along with the drama, but instead tries to calm things down. For example, if one of your friends shares gossip with you, instead of listening to it and saying nothing, try saying, "Hey, I'm trying to get better about not gossiping and causing drama. I wouldn't want others whispering about me, so I think we should work on not whispering about others."

Most friendships will experience drama from time to time, but some friendships have more than their fair share. If you have a friend who has a bad habit of being dishonest and causing quarrels or a friend who gossips frequently and separates close friends, it might be time to take a break or even quit the drama club. Drama can stir up all kinds of emotions and take your focus off more important things—like your true friends, your family, and most importantly, God.

Think About It

Have you ever experienced drama
with a friend or a group of friends?

Talk About It

Questions to ask your mom:

When you were my age, what kind of drama did you experience with your friends?

_____

_____

_____

_____

_____

_____

Tell me about a time when dishonesty caused a quarrel or gossip separated close friends.

Were you ever the one causing the drama?

Questions for your mom to ask you:

Have you experienced drama with any of your friends?

_____

_____

_____

_____

Can you think of a time when dishonesty caused a quarrel or gossip separated close friends? Tell me about what happened.

_____

_____

_____

Have you ever been the one who caused the drama?

This Week

Be on the lookout for times this week when you are tempted to start drama by being dishonest or gossiping. A good remedy for breaking the habit is to catch yourself when you are tempted and act the opposite way. For example, if you are tempted to lie or exaggerate (both are dishonest), tell the truth instead. If you are tempted to gossip about someone, catch yourself and say something nice about the person instead. To break a bad habit, you have to substitute it with a new and better habit.

Keep Going

Write down a peacemaker response for each situation below:

"Did you hear about the text Anna Grace sent to Natalie? She called Sydney a bad name, and Sydney found out about it."

Your response:

_____

_____

"I heard that Brooke flunked the test and her mom grounded her from going to the party."

Your response:

_____

_____

"Avery is always bragging about how rich her family is, and it's so annoying."

Your response:

_____

_____

Week 7:
Taking Home the Prize

Bible Reading

Trust in the LORD and do what is good; dwell in the land and live securely. Take delight in the LORD, and He will give you your heart's desires.
—Psalm 37:3-4

Read the passage aloud and listen carefully for the answers to the following questions:

We can live securely if we do what?

_____

_____

God will give us our heart's desires if we do what?

_____

_____

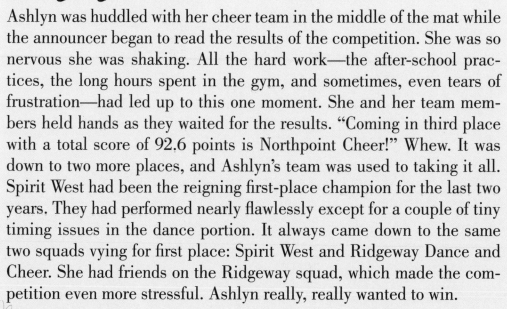

Bringing It Home

Ashlyn was huddled with her cheer team in the middle of the mat while the announcer began to read the results of the competition. She was so nervous she was shaking. All the hard work—the after-school practices, the long hours spent in the gym, and sometimes, even tears of frustration—had led up to this one moment. She and her team members held hands as they waited for the results. "Coming in third place with a total score of 92.6 points is Northpoint Cheer!" Whew. It was down to two more places, and Ashlyn's team was used to taking it all. Spirit West had been the reigning first-place champion for the last two years. They had performed nearly flawlessly except for a couple of tiny timing issues in the dance portion. It always came down to the same two squads vying for first place: Spirit West and Ridgeway Dance and Cheer. She had friends on the Ridgeway squad, which made the competition even more stressful. Ashlyn really, really wanted to win.

"Coming in second place . . ." Ashlyn held her breath and hoped the announcer would announce the other team's name, which would mean

she and her teammates had for sure taken home the prize again. She squeezed her teammates' hands and said a silent prayer to God: *Please, please, God, let us win.* The announcer continued, "With a total score of 94.8—is Spirit West. First place goes to Ridgeway Dance and Cheer with a total score of 95.2!"

Wait, what?! Ashlyn thought. She desperately tried to mentally rewind what the announcer had just said. *Did I hear that right?* When the team next to her team jumped to their feet and began screaming and hugging one another, she knew she had her answer. Ashlyn was stunned. Sure, second place was great, but her team wasn't used to getting second place. She watched as her coach and team captain went up to receive the award. *Did God not hear my prayer?* thought Ashlyn. *Doesn't the Bible say He will give me the desires of my heart?*

What does God's Word say?

It's perfectly normal to want God to grant our heart's desires. Sometimes Psalm 37:3–4 can be misunderstood to mean that whatever we want, God will give it to us. Not true. The verse says to "take delight in the Lord." We may be disappointed when something we desire doesn't happen, but we can trust that God is still good. That is why it's important to seek God and build our relationship with Him. When disappointments come, we can take delight in the fact that God is still in control on His throne and desires to have a relationship with us.

Besides, who needs a first-place trophy when God is the real grand prize? Delight in Him, and His desires will become your desires.

Think About It

Is it hard for you to "take delight in the Lord" even when things don't go your way?

Talk About It

Questions to ask your mom:

Can you think of a time when you asked God to give you a "desire of your heart" and He didn't answer the prayer in the way you had hoped? What happened?

Was it hard for you to trust Him at the time?

_____

_____

What do you do to "take delight in the Lord"?

_____

_____

Questions for your mom to ask you:

Can you think of a time when you asked God to give you a "desire of your heart" and He didn't answer the prayer in the way you had hoped? What happened?

_____

_____

_____

In the situation above, what might be some reasons God did not grant Ashlyn's request to get first place in the cheer competition?

_____

_____

_____

_____

_____

What might God's "desire" be for the other team that hasn't won in years?

_____

_____

_____

_____

If Ashlyn was more focused on delighting in the Lord and His desires had become her desires, how might that have helped her in her disappointment?

_____

_____

_____

This Week

Pray and ask God to help you "take delight in the Lord" when things don't go your way.

Keep Going

Make a list below of your "desires":

1. _____

2. _____

3. _____

4. _____

5. _____

Now, make a list of ways you can "take delight in the Lord."

1. _____

2. _____

3. _____

4. _____

5. _____

Week 8:
Jealousy Versus Joy

Bible Reading

A tranquil heart is life to the body, but jealousy is rottenness to the bones.

—Proverbs 14:30

Read the passage aloud and listen carefully for the answers to the following questions:

What kind of heart is "life to the body"?

_____

What causes "rottenness to the bones"?

_____

Bringing It Home

It had taken over a year of begging and pleading, but finally, Samantha's parents gave in. She was allowed to engage in social media—under her parents' watchful eyes, of course. Her friends had been on social media for a year or more, so she could hardly wait to join the party. Only one problem: Samantha quickly learned that the party wasn't always fun, and sometimes, you weren't even invited.

At first, she loved the ability to interact with her friends on social media. She didn't have to wait until a friend came over to ask her opinion about a new outfit or borrow her mom's phone to text her friends a picture of her dog dressed up in his Halloween costume. Now she could post real-time and talk to her friends on the spot. Who wouldn't love that, right? Wrong. After several months of being on social media, Samantha began to feel jealousy creeping in when she looked at her friends' pictures and status updates.

Sometimes it happened when a friend posted and tagged other friends, but then didn't tag her. Other times it was a group shot of some of her friends who had gotten together and not included her. Or maybe it was over a picture of a friend who got a lot of positive comments and praises. Samantha's pictures never seemed to get as many "likes" and comments. She thought about sharing her feelings with her mother, but she was afraid her parents would make her get off social media if they knew it was upsetting her. Samantha knew she needed to make some changes to limit the amount of time she spent at the virtual party, so she asked God to help her take the step.

What does God's Word say?

Everyone struggles with jealousy from time to time, but in a world of constant connectivity, it seems the battle to fight it off is never-ending. No wonder God says, "A tranquil heart is life to the body." If you look up the word *tranquil*, its definition is "free from disturbing emotions," "peaceful," "quiet," or "calm." When we expose ourselves to situations that rob our hearts of tranquility, it will affect our lives as a whole.

I'm not saying that we should give up social media completely. It will always be around, but that doesn't mean we have to engage it around the clock. We need to recognize when it becomes too much for our souls to handle and pull away when we find that it is disturbing our emotions. Sometimes the best thing we can do to have a tranquil heart is to take a break. Maybe that means only allowing yourself a scheduled amount of time each day to interact on social media or only getting on certain days of the week. Maybe that means removing all notifications from your phone so you are not bombarded with reminders throughout the day. And for some, it may mean getting off altogether if it proves to be too much for your soul to handle.

Girls who learn to take charge of technology will guard against negative emotions like jealousy, loneliness, and hurt feelings before they begin to take over and eat away at their souls. Don't forget to go to God and share your emotions. Ask Him to help you guard your heart so that it is filled with peace and calm, rather than jealousy and other negative emotions. Also, share your feelings with your parents. When we are honest about our negative emotions, we don't feel as alone in the struggle.

Think About It

Do you struggle with jealousy?

Talk About It

Questions to ask your mom:

When you were my age, did you struggle with jealousy? If so, what kinds of things triggered it?

_____

_____

_____

_____

Do you ever find yourself struggling with jealousy now, especially when you are on social media? If so, share an example.

_____

_____

_____

_____

Questions for your mom to ask you:

Is jealousy a problem for you and your friends when it comes to social media? How so?

_____

_____

_____

_____

What are some steps you can take to help guard against jealousy when you are on social media?

_____

_____

_____

_____

Do you feel comfortable coming to me about your emotions? If no, why not?

_____

_____

_____

_____

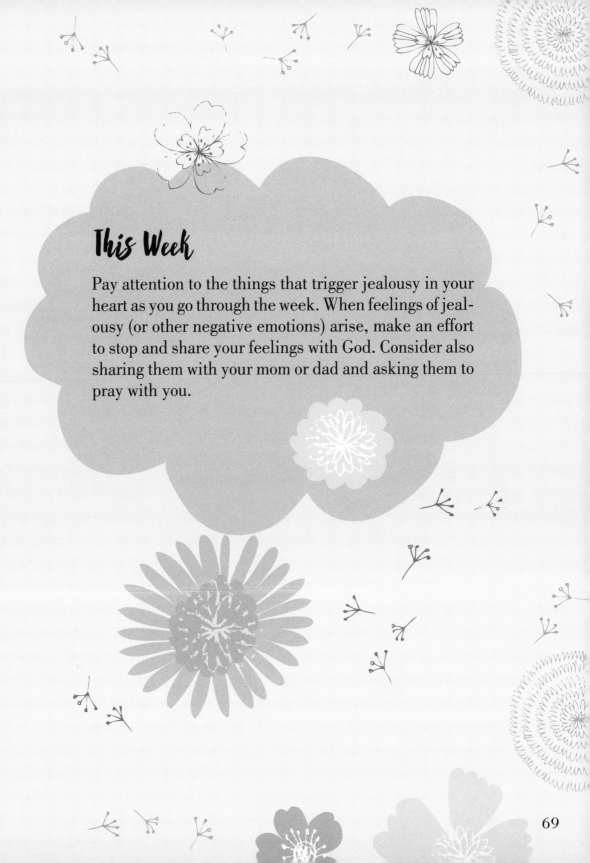

This Week

Pay attention to the things that trigger jealousy in your heart as you go through the week. When feelings of jealousy (or other negative emotions) arise, make an effort to stop and share your feelings with God. Consider also sharing them with your mom or dad and asking them to pray with you.

Keep Going

Finish the sentences below:

I feel jealous when

_____

_____

_____

My heart feels at peace when

_____

_____

_____

Week 9:
One Step at a Time

Bible Reading

I am sure of this, that He who started a good work in you will carry it on to completion until the day of Christ Jesus.
—Philippians 1:6

Read the passage aloud and listen carefully for the answers to the following questions:

Who started a "good work in you"?

_____

_____

God will carry the good work on to what?

_____

_____

_____

Bringing It Home

Brenna sat in her room, grounded for the third time this week. The first time, when her mom had told her to change the TV channel because the show she was watching used a bad word, Brenna had been guilty of rolling her eyes. The second time, she'd complained about the breakfast her dad had cooked and said she wished she could put it in the trash and eat a Pop-Tart instead. And now, here she was back in her room again, this time for screaming at her sister for taking her favorite blanket out of her room and curling up on the couch with it. Oh, and as a bonus, Brenna had grabbed the corner of the blanket and ripped it out from under her sister, causing her to tumble onto the floor.

Honestly, she knew she was wrong all three times. She had been selfish, rude, and just plain mean. She knew the Bible said we all would sin and fall short of the glory of God (Romans 3:23), but wow, she was going overtime on the sinning part this week. She always felt bad when

she sinned and would eventually apologize to her parents. Her sister was harder to apologize to, but still—she knew she needed to do it.

As she sat in her room thinking about it, she wondered why God was so patient with her when she sinned so much. It brought tears to her eyes to think about how He paid for her sins when He died on the cross. She loved Jesus and wanted to live for Him, but sometimes it was so hard. As a Christian, shouldn't she be further along in her journey of faith? When would she stop being such a sinner?

What does God's Word say?

Our Christian lives are like a long-distance race. Sometimes we will perform well, and sometimes we will stumble and fall. God loves us no matter where we are in the race, and He knows we will sometimes get off course and act in ways that aren't very Christlike. Realizing that truth should cause us to love Him even more. He doesn't expect us to be perfect. When Jesus died on the cross for our sins, He knew we would still sin; and yet He still chose to die for us.

We are all works in progress. You, me, your mom, your dad, your Sunday school teacher—every one of us. Like a precious painting on a canvas, God will continue to work on us throughout our lives until the masterpiece is complete. A brush stroke here, a new color there . . . The picture won't be perfect until we stand face-to-face with Jesus. The important thing is that we move forward and not backward in our journey because that shows progress. Progress may look like two steps forward and one step back, but it's still progress all the same. As long as we are sorry when we sin and we do what we can to get back on track (confess, apologize, and make it right), we are still moving forward in the race.

Think About It

Are you easy on yourself when you make mistakes?

Talk About It

Questions to ask your mom:

Can you think of a time when you sinned and wondered if you had messed up too much for God to forgive you? (Your mom will have to decide if she feels comfortable sharing about the sin.)

Did you take steps to get back on track (confess, apologize, and make it right)?

_____

_____

_____

How does it make you feel to know you are a work in progress?

_____

_____

Questions for your mom to ask you:

Can you think of a time when you sinned and wondered if you had messed up too much for God to forgive you?

_____

_____

_____

Did you take steps to get back on track (confess, apologize, and make it right)?

_____

_____

_____

How does it make you feel to know you are a work in progress?

_____

_____

_____

This Week

Be on the lookout for times when you stumble and sin. Catch yourself (even if it's after the fact!), and take steps to get back on track. Take a minute to pray and thank God for His patience with us when we sin.

Keep Going

Read back over Brenna's story and the three ways she sinned. In each situation, write down what she could do to get back on track (without waiting for her parents to make her do it!).

Sin #1: Rolling her eyes at her mom (bad, disrespectful attitude):

_____

_____

_____

Sin #2: Complaining about the meal her dad cooked (rude and cruel):

_____

_____

_____

Sin #3: Screaming at her sister and pulling the blanket out from under her (selfish and unloving):

_____

_____

_____

Week 10:
One of a Kind

Bible Reading

Woe to the one who argues with his Maker—one clay pot among many. Does clay say to the one forming it, "What are you making?" Or does your work say, "He has no hands"?

—Isaiah 45:9

Read the passage aloud and listen carefully for the answers to the following questions:

Woe to the one who argues with whom?

_____

What question does it say the clay asks his maker?

_____

_____

Bringing It Home

Kelsey sat at the lunch table and watched her friends at a nearby table laughing and cutting up. They would have gladly welcomed her at the table, but she couldn't because of a peanut allergy. Even the tiniest bite of nut could be a danger to her health. She knew it wouldn't be fair for the school to ban everyone else from bringing their yummy peanut butter and jelly sandwiches, but she also didn't think it was fair to have to sit at a special table reserved for the students with allergies.

None of her friends were at the table, and the other kids at the table seemed to have someone they could talk to. She was so lonely. Tears filled in her eyes as she glanced over at her friends' table, and one of them waved and gave her a sad face. Lunch was supposed to be fun, but Kelsey hated it even more than gym class. Why did God make her with this stupid allergy? It wasn't fair.

What does God's Word say?

The Bible says a lot about God creating us to be special and unique. He could have made us all exactly alike, but that would be so boring! Everyone has something about themselves they wish they could change. Some girls wish they were taller or shorter. Others wish they could be heavier or thinner. Some wish they had straight hair while others wish they had curly hair. Others have allergies or disabilities that make life harder. And yet, God created each and every one of us with differences and for unique purposes.

We may not understand why God created us in the way He did, but we are to be grateful all the same. He is the Potter and we are the clay. Imagine if you were molding a cup out of modeling clay for fun and when you were done, the clay cup spoke up and complained, "What do you think you're doing?! I didn't want to be a cup! I wanted to be a bowl!" Okay, after freaking out and hiding under your bed because a blob of clay had started talking to you, you would probably feel unappreciated after spending so much time on your creation. You're in charge, so who is the cup to question the maker?

God feels the same way when we question His creation. He wants us to come to Him when we're feeling frustrated or sad about something, but He also wants us to trust Him when it comes to the person He created us to be.

Think About It

Does God owe us an explanation or reason when it comes to the way He created us?

Talk About It

Questions to ask your mom:

Have you ever wished God made you differently? If so, how?

After reading the verse, do you feel differently now? Why or why not?

_____

_____

_____

_____

Questions for your mom to ask you:

When was the last time you complained to your Maker about the way He created you? (Even if you didn't speak the complaint out loud, remember: He knows your thoughts!) What did you complain about?

_____

_____

_____

_____

What can God teach us through difficulties like allergies, flaws, or disabilities?

This Week

Be on the lookout this week for times when you grumble or complain about something you don't like about yourself. Instead of complaining, catch yourself and tell God you trust Him even if you don't understand the reason behind it.

Keep Going

Think about Kelsey's story. What might God's purpose be in allowing her to have a peanut allergy? (Check all the apply.)

_____ It might make her more likely to reach out to other kids who have allergies and often feel lonely.

_____ Maybe there is someone at the table that God wants her to get to know.

_____ It might remind her that everyone has weaknesses, even if you can't always see them.

_____ It might help her grow in her relationship with God because she will depend on Him more in times of need.

_____ God doesn't really care about things like allergies. He's got more important things to do.

_____ God probably wants to punish her for something she did.

How Did You Do?

If you checked all but the last two, you are right on target!

Week 11:
Better Than Gold

Bible Reading

A good name is to be chosen over great wealth; favor is better than silver and gold.

—Proverbs 22:1

Read the passage aloud and listen carefully for the answers to the following questions:

A good name is to be chosen over what?

_____

What is better than silver and gold?

_____

Bringing It Home

"Do I have to invite her to my party?" Grace asked her mom. She and Laney had been friends since preschool, but they weren't hanging out as much now. The last few times Grace had gone to her house, Laney was bossy and wouldn't do anything Grace wanted to do. They watched the movie Laney wanted to watch, ate the snacks Laney wanted to eat, and played the board games Laney wanted to play after the movie. Oh, and when Laney started to lose the game, she said she was tired and wanted to quit. It was so annoying.

In preschool, Laney was the girl who shared the cookie in her lunch and took turns being "it" when playing tag on the playground. Now she was the girl no one wanted to hang out with because she was bossy and selfish. Grace knew she needed to show love to Laney, but honestly, it was getting harder and harder to be her friend.

What does God's Word say?

Everyone has a reputation or a few words that others close to them would use to describe them. If you were asked to describe each of your friends in three words, what kind of words might you choose? What words might others use to describe you? Are you known as "the smart girl," "the nice girl," "the rude girl," "the bossy girl," or "the sweet girl"? If you were given a name (or words to describe you), would it be a good name or a bad name?

God's Word reminds us that a good name is better than being wealthy, and favor is more valuable than silver and gold. Tell that to some of the celebrities who don't seem to care much about having a good name or reputation! The best way to have a good name or reputation is to strive to be like Jesus. The Bible tells us to be "imitators of God" (Ephesians 5:1). Going to church doesn't necessarily make you like God, just as climbing into your pet Fido's doghouse doesn't make you a dog. What's important is to work at being like Jesus and treating others as He treated them. Those who truly follow Christ can't help but have a good name and reputation.

Think About It

Do you think you have a "good name" among your friends and classmates?

Talk About It

Questions to ask your mom:

When you were in elementary school, what was your reputation?

_____

_____

_____

_____

What about middle and high school?

_____

_____

_____

_____

Did your reputation change? If so, why do you think it changed?

_____

_____

_____

_____

_____

_____

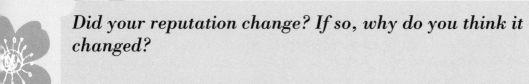

Questions for your mom to ask you:

What three words might your friends choose if they were asked to describe you?

_____

_____

_____

_____

_____

_____

What are some areas you might need to work on to improve your reputation and be more like Jesus?

This Week

Be on the lookout for people you know who have a good name or reputation. Make an effort to pay a compliment to one of them by bringing up one of the qualities that give them a good name.

Keep Going

Unscramble the words below. Each one is a quality Jesus had that we should imitate in order to have a good name or reputation.

nikd: __ __ __ __

nivgig: __ __ __ __ __ __

behmul: __ __ __ __ __ __

atenipt: __ __ __ __ __ __ __

rgifnovig: __ __ __ __ __ __ __ __ __

Week 12:
Whatever . . .

Bible Reading

Finally brothers, whatever is true, whatever is honorable, whatever is just, whatever is pure, whatever is lovely, whatever is commendable—if there is any moral excellence and if there is any praise— dwell on these things.
—Philippians 4:8

Read the passage aloud and listen carefully for the answers to the following questions:

What word did you hear repeated in the verse?

_____

What does the passage tell us to do with all those "whatevers"?

_____

Bringing It Home

Kendall squirmed as Meredith pushed Play on the movie. It was PG-13, and Kendall was pretty sure her parents wouldn't want her watching it. She had been so excited about spending the night with Meredith and didn't want to ruin the fun by telling her she couldn't watch the movie. About fifteen minutes into the movie and three cuss words later, Kendall knew she needed to say something. She worked up her courage and told Meredith she didn't feel like watching the movie any longer and wanted to play a game. Meredith pushed her to keep watching, and finally Kendall broke down and told her the truth. "I'm really not allowed to watch PG-13 movies without my parents' permission. They don't want me watching movies with bad language and other bad stuff in them."

But Meredith wouldn't take no for an answer. "Seriously? I've seen this movie like a million times, and it's not that bad. I promise. I've seen way worse movies than this." Kendall had a choice to make and was silent for a minute while she thought about her situation. "Well, if you really want to watch the movie, I guess I can call my mom and tell her to come get me. I really want to stay, but I don't want to disobey my parents." Meredith got up and turned the TV off. "Fine. I'll watch it later. What game do you want to play?"

Whew, that was close, thought Kendall. She had a feeling this wouldn't be the last time she had to make a tough choice like this.

What does God's Word say?

God gives us six "whatevers" to guide us when it comes to making choices about what we watch and listen to and how we should behave. Whatever is true, honorable, just, pure, lovely, and commendable—and then the verse adds "if there is any moral excellence and if there is any praise—dwell on these things." Things that are pure and good are "moral" and pleasing to God, and He wants us to think often of these types of things.

As you get older, you will be tempted at times to take part in things that are not moral and that turn your time and attention away from God. It may not seem like a big deal to listen to songs that have bad language or watch shows or video clips that show inappropriate situations, but God calls us to live a pure life. He gives us the "whatevers" to test situations as they come up and make choices that would be pleasing to Him. You've heard it said, "Garbage in, garbage out," and it's true. If you allow bad things to enter your heart, after a while, they will begin to overflow into your actions and thoughts. Many of your friends will make the wrong choice and say "whatever" when faced with temptation, but God calls believers to remember the "whatevers" instead.

Think About It

Is it hard for you to do the right thing when you are in a tempting situation?

Talk About It

Questions to ask your mom:

Can you think of a time when you were tempted to participate in something that wasn't pleasing to God and it left you feeling distant from Him?

What are some things you do to "dwell" on the six "whatevers"?

_____

_____

_____

_____

_____

Questions for your mom to ask you:

Can you think of a time when you were tempted to participate in something that wasn't pleasing to God, and you had to choose between following God or following the crowd? What was the situation and what did you choose?

_____

_____

_____

_____

What are some things you can think about or dwell on that are pleasing to God?

This Week

Pay attention to the influences around you (shows you watch, music you listen to, apps you download, conversations you have, etc.) and test them out with the six "whatevers." If something doesn't pass the test, turn it off and turn to God instead.

Keep Going

Look in a dictionary to find the following six "whatevers" in order to better understand what each one means. Write the definition below each one.

True:

_____

Honorable:

_____

Just:

_____

Pure:

_____

Lovely:

_____

Commendable:

_____

Week 13:
Tough Times

Bible Reading

Consider it a great joy, my brothers, whenever you experience various trials, knowing that the testing of your faith produces endurance. But endurance must do its complete work, so that you may be mature and complete, lacking nothing.
—James 1:2-4

Read the passage aloud and listen carefully for the answers to the following questions:

We should consider it a great joy when we experience what?

_____

What produces endurance?

_____

Bringing It Home

Paige didn't see it coming. One day she was hanging out with her best friend, Amelia, and the next day, Amelia was calling to tell her she was moving. Paige knew it wasn't the end of the world, but it was the end of her world since Amelia was her only friend at school. Paige had been the new girl a few months ago, and it had taken her awhile to find a friend. Night after night she prayed and asked God to give her just one special friend to help with the loneliness. One day, Amelia had plopped her lunch tray down beside her and asked if she could sit at the table. All the other girls had their little friend groups, and Paige didn't feel welcome at their tables. Sitting alone had been hard, so she knew Amelia was an answer to her prayer for a friend.

And now her one friend was moving. She knew she needed to be there for Amelia to support her in her move, but she needed support too. She wanted to turn to God for help, but she didn't understand why He would allow this to happen to her. Did He even care that her heart was broken?

What does God's Word say?

Trials (or difficulties) are a part of life for everyone. No one can escape them. God didn't plan for us to walk through our trials alone. Nor did He promise to rescue us from our trials. The world is an imperfect place, and until we get to heaven, we will experience things that can sometimes make trusting God difficult. No matter what, we can trust that God cares when we are going through a trial.

God doesn't want our trials to go to waste. The Bible tells us they can serve a purpose and actually make our faith (belief in God) even stronger. Trials can produce *endurance*, which means "the ability or strength to continue or last." Many Christians trust God when things are going great, but the true test of our faith is whether we will still trust Him when things aren't going great. If we continue to trust God when we go through tough times, it will produce a lasting faith that can weather any storm of life.

Think About It

Is it hard for you to trust God when you experience trials?

Talk About It

Questions to ask your mom:

Can you think of a trial you have experienced in your life that made your faith in God stronger? What was it?

_____

_____

_____

_____

At the time, did you realize the difficulty was building your faith?

_____

_____

_____

_____

Questions for your mom to ask you:

What trials have you experienced?

_____

_____

_____

_____

Why do you think some people turn away from God when they experience difficulties?

_____

_____

_____

_____

Be on the lookout for someone experiencing a trial. Think of something kind you can do to help lighten her load. Pray that God will use the trial to strengthen her faith.

Keep Going

Remember that *endurance* means "the ability or strength to continue or last." Just as trials can produce endurance in the lives of Christians, how do the following build endurance?

A marathon runner:

_____

A straight-A student:

_____

An Olympic gymnast:

_____

A spelling-bee champion:

_____

The Energizer Bunny:

_____

Week 14:
Be Happy!

Bible Reading

How happy is the man who does not follow the advice of the wicked or take the path of sinners or join a group of mockers! Instead, his delight is in the LORD's instruction, and he meditates on it day and night.

—Psalm 1:1-2

Read the passage aloud and listen carefully for the answers to the following questions:

The man who does not follow the advice of the wicked or take the path of sinners is what?

_____

His delight is in the Lord's what?

_____

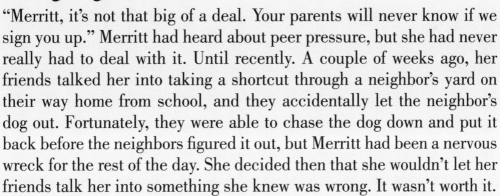

Bringing It Home

"Merritt, it's not that big of a deal. Your parents will never know if we sign you up." Merritt had heard about peer pressure, but she had never really had to deal with it. Until recently. A couple of weeks ago, her friends talked her into taking a shortcut through a neighbor's yard on their way home from school, and they accidentally let the neighbor's dog out. Fortunately, they were able to chase the dog down and put it back before the neighbors figured it out, but Merritt had been a nervous wreck for the rest of the day. She decided then that she wouldn't let her friends talk her into something she knew was wrong. It wasn't worth it.

But here she was again, and it was harder than she'd expected to find the words to stand up for what was right. She had looked forward to the sleepover, but all the girls wanted to do was hang out on Sloan's mom's laptop. Several of them had social media accounts, but Merritt's parents didn't feel like she was old enough to have one yet. You were supposed to be older to get on the sites, but her friends had lied about

their ages to get on, and now they were trying to convince her to do the same thing. "You don't have to put in your real name. It's so much fun and eveeeeeeryone is on the site but you."

Merritt knew that wasn't true, but sometimes it was so hard to do the right thing. She knew if she didn't, she would continue to find herself in tempting situations that would only lead to trouble. She didn't like to disobey her parents' rules, but at the same time, she wanted to fit in with her friends. Ugh, what was she going to do?

What does God's Word say?

God knew we would be tempted here on this earth, so He's not the least bit surprised when it happens. We all have a sinful nature (a desire to do things that are wrong), and that's why God wants us to delight in His instruction (the Bible) and meditate (read, study, and think about it) day and night. Then, when we are tempted, we will be more likely to remember what God has to say about the situation and have the strength to do the right thing.

God warns us about following the advice of the wicked and taking the path of sinners because He knows it won't lead to happiness in the end. If you find yourself in a situation where, like Merritt, your friends are tempting you to do the wrong things, it might be a good idea to find a new group of friends. A real friend will not pressure you to do the wrong thing or make fun of you taking delight in the Lord's instruction. Ever.

Think About It

What do you think you would have
done if you had been in Merritt's situation?
(Be honest!)

Talk About It

Questions to ask your mom:

*Can you think of a time when you experienced peer pressure
to do something wrong and you "took the path of sinners"?
What happened?*

Can you think of a time when you didn't follow peer pressure but instead took delight in the Lord's instruction (and did the right thing)? What happened?

_____

_____

_____

_____

_____

Questions for your mom to ask you:

Can you think of a time when your friends tried to put pressure on you to do something wrong and you were tempted to join them? What happened?

_____

_____

_____

_____

Why do you think the man "who does not follow the advice of the wicked or take the path of sinners" is "happy"?

This Week

As you go through this next week, pay attention to situations when a person "follows the path of sinners." Maybe it's in a book you're reading for school. Or on a show you watch. Or in a song you love to play. Or possibly even in real life. In each situation, what is the right response?

Keep Going

This week, take some time each day to read through Psalm 119. Have your mom do it too, or possibly even do it together. (Warning: It's 176 verses, but don't let that scare you off! If you divide it up, you will only have to read about twenty-five verses each day.) Every time you read a verse that talks about taking delight in or meditating on God's . . .

commands

decrees

statutes

instructions

word

judgments

. . . highlight it or underline it in your Bible. Try to read the psalm slowly, and take time to let the words soak in. By reading it throughout the week, you are "delighting in the Lord's instruction" and "meditating on it day and night." Good job!

Week 15:
The Remedy for Worry

Bible Reading

Don't worry about anything, but in everything, through prayer and petition with thanksgiving, let your requests be made known to God. And the peace of God, which surpasses every thought, will guard your hearts and minds in Christ Jesus.
—Philippians 4:6–7

Read the passage aloud and listen carefully for the answers to the following questions:

God's Word tells us not to worry about what?

_____

What should we do when we worry?

_____

What will guard our hearts and minds?

_____

Bringing It Home

Three more days until the big family vacation. Emma should have been excited about her first-ever trip to Disney World, but now, thanks to her best friend, Olivia, all she could think about was the plane ride. She had never been on a plane before, and when she told Olivia about her trip and getting to fly on an airplane for the first time, Olivia asked her if she was worried about the plane crashing. "What? That doesn't really ever happen," Emma responded, hoping to change the subject. But Olivia didn't take the hint and started going on and on about a news story she heard and blah . . . blah . . . blah. Emma hadn't been worried about the plane ride until she talked to Olivia. Actually, she'd been excited. But now it was hard to feel excited when all she could think about was what Olivia had told her.

As she lay in her bed that night thinking about it, she wondered what she should do. Should she say something to her mom about how scared she was? She had tried all day to forget about the conversation with Olivia, but she just couldn't. She was near tears when all of a sudden, she heard her bedroom door creak open. Her mom appeared at her bedside. "Hey, honey, you seemed pretty quiet at dinner tonight when we were talking about the big trip. Is everything okay?" Without thinking, Emma burst into tears and told her mother about what Olivia had said at lunch. She confessed to her mother that it was hard to be excited about the trip because she was so worried about the plane ride. Emma's mother hugged her tight and told her that there was nothing to worry about. She also told her that riding in a plane is safer than riding in a car. *Wow!* thought Emma. *Why didn't Olivia tell me that little fact?*

Before Emma's mother left the room, she suggested they pray and talk to God about her worries. As Emma's mother closed the prayer, she asked God to give Emma a peace about the trip and especially the plane ride. The next morning, Emma woke up excited about her big family vacation once again. God had everything under control, and Emma felt at peace. Only two more days until vacation!

What does God's Word say?

When we worry, God's Word tells us to turn to Him immediately with prayer and petition. If you look up the word *petition*, you'll find it means "a request made for something desired." God wants us to bring our requests to Him, but He also wants us to include something else in our prayers: thanksgiving. God knows that when we take the time to express our thanks to Him, it takes the focus off our worry and puts it on His trustworthiness.

We can trust that God hears our prayers and knows our desires. He may not answer our prayers exactly in the way we had hoped, but He can always be trusted, no matter what. When we practice praying and talking to God whenever we begin to worry, it will strengthen the bond we have with Him. He promises to give us "peace which surpasses (or is greater than) every thought." His peace stands guard over our hearts and refuses to let worry come in. Yet, in order to have that peace, we have to trust God with whatever is bothering us by handing our worries over to Him.

Think About It

Do you struggle with worry?

Talk About It

Questions to ask your mom:

Can you tell me about a worry you had when you were my age?

On a scale of 1–10, with 10 being the greatest, how worried were you? Did you tell your mom or dad?

_____

_____

_____

Did you pray about it at the time?

_____

Questions for your mom to ask you:

Can you share something you were recently worried about?

_____

_____

_____

Did you pray about it at the time?

_____

This Week

Catch yourself every time you begin to worry, and apply this prayer remedy:

1. Pray right away. (You don't have to pray out loud for God to hear you!)

2. Tell God why you are worried, and petition Him for help. Ask for His peace.

3. Thank Him for always being there and hearing your requests.

Repeat steps 1–3 every time you begin to worry again. Each time, picture yourself handing your worry over to God.

Keep Going

Choose the remedy for each of the worries below. Check the right answer.

1. The spelling test is tomorrow, and you studied every night this week. You are worried you won't pass because spelling is your weakest subject. You . . .

    ___ a. keep worrying about flunking the test until your stomach hurts.

    ___ b. stop and pray about it. You tell God (petition) that you want to make a good grade because you studied hard, and you thank Him (thanksgiving) for being there for you. If you don't pass, it's not the end of the world.

2. Tryouts for the school play are tomorrow, and you are worried you won't get the part you are auditioning for: You . . .

    ___ a. toss and turn all night. You can't stop thinking about it.

    ___ b. tell God (petition) that you really want the part you are auditioning for and end your prayer by thanking Him (thanksgiving) for the answer in advance. Even if you get a different part, you know you can trust Him.

3. You just got braces, and you worry about the boys in your class teasing you. You . . .

    ___ a. worry in the car all the way to school and consider telling your mom you are sick and need to stay home.

    ___ b. pray on the way to school. Again, for the millionth time. You ask God (petition) for a big dose of His peace and thank Him (thanksgiving) for walking into school with you. Even if the boys tease you, God is there to help you survive it.

How Did You Do?

If you answered *b* more than once, you chose the right remedy. Keep up the good work!

If you chose *a* more than once, you need to work harder at turning to God immediately in prayer when you begin to worry. Practice makes perfect!

Week 16:
First Things First

Bible Reading

Do not make an idol for yourself, whether in the shape of anything in the heavens above or on the earth below or in the waters under the earth. You must not bow down to them or worship them.

—Exodus 20:4-5

121

Read the passage aloud and listen carefully for the answers to the following questions:

What does God tell us not to make for ourselves?

_____

_____

What does God tell us not to bow down to or worship?

_____

_____

Bringing It Home

Jenna couldn't remember when soccer hadn't been a part of her life. She had been playing the sport since she was in preschool and had a wall filled with team pictures to prove it. Trophies lined her bookshelves, and her dad had joked that he would have to build another one since there wasn't any room on the first one for another trophy. Jenna liked having something she was good at. And according to her coaches, she was good. Really good. Last year, she tried out for a competitive soccer team and made it. Many of the competitions were out of town, and she loved spending time with her parents and the other team members and their families in hotels, especially if it was warm enough to swim in the hotel pool.

Soccer was Jenna's life. And that was the problem. Somewhere along the way, soccer had become more important to Jenna and her family than their relationship with Christ. At first, Jenna and her parents tried to find a church to attend on Sunday mornings when they were out of town for soccer games, but after a while, it was too much trouble and she was wiped out from being on the field the day before. Her mom tried doing a devotional on the way home from the out-of-town games, but it always seemed like she was trying to squeeze it in so she could check if off a to-do list.

Jenna had been going to the same church since she was little and missed seeing her church friends on Sunday mornings. Many of them were doing church activities together or hanging out on the weekends, and sometimes Jenna felt left out and no longer a part of the group. She was still invited to all the church activities, but soccer was her first priority. Recently, she had overheard her parents having a talk about how they needed to make their relationship with Christ their first priority, and if they couldn't find a way to do that while traveling out of town, something would need to change. Jenna wasn't sure how she felt about it. She loved soccer, but at the same time, she felt distant in her relationship with God.

What does God's Word say?

The definition of the word *idol* is "any person or thing regarded with blind admiration, adoration, or devotion." If you are devoted to something, you give it your time and attention. It's not a bad thing to give something our admiration, adoration, and devotion, as long as it doesn't steal our attention away from time that God deserves. When something becomes more important to us than our relationship with Christ, it becomes an idol.

In Bible times, people would often bow down to idols that they thought had healing powers. Sometimes the idol was a silly carved statue, or in one case, a golden calf. They danced and chanted and begged the idols or false gods to help them. Imagine how silly that must have looked. We may not see people worshipping idols like that today, but we have

our own modern-day idols that steal our attention away from God. Some people worship money or name-brand clothes. Other people worship their smartphones, a celebrity, or even a sport they play—the way Jenna and her family began to "worship" soccer more than God. We can be devoted to other things, but Christ should always be our number-one affection. When He's not, it's time to make some changes.

Think About It

Can you think of an idol you have had in your life that you worshipped more than God?

Talk About It

Questions to ask your mom:

Have you ever had an idol in your life that became more important to you than your relationship with Christ? (We all have, so the answer is probably yes.) What was it?

_____

_____

_____

What are some things that grown-ups worship (other than God)?

What do you do to make sure Christ remains your number-one affection/love? (Or what do you plan to do if He's not?)

Questions for your mom to ask you:

What are some common idols girls your age worship?

What do you do to make sure Christ remains your number-one affection/love? (Or what do you plan to do if He's not?)

_____

_____

_____

_____

_____

This Week

Practice making Christ your number-one affection/love this week by spending time with Him each day. We get to know Christ by reading our Bibles and talking to Him in prayer. When you pray, talk to Him like you would talk to one of your close friends. Be careful not to make it all about you, and spend time telling God what you love about Him.

Keep Going

Which of the following comments sounds like it could be describing idol worship?

"I'm obsessed with her. I would sell everything I own to get tickets to her concert. I have downloaded all of her songs and know every word to every song. If I ever met her in person, I would probably pass out. I love her so much!"

Idol alert? Yes   or   No

"My friends are super important to me, and I love spending time with them. But I try to make sure I spend time with Christ during the week, since He's the most important relationship in my life."

Idol alert? Yes   or   No

"I don't really have time for church or reading my Bible because I'm always studying. I have to make the honor roll each month. It's all I think about."

Idol alert? Yes   or   No

"I can't remember the last time I opened my Bible or prayed. Now that I have my own tablet, I spend most of my time playing games or watching my favorite shows."

Idol alert? Yes   or   No

"I love being on a dance team, but if it gets in the way of church or my Bible study group during the week, it has to go."

Idol alert? Yes   or   No

Week 17:
Inside-Out

Bible Reading

A good man produces good out of the good storeroom of his heart. An evil man produces evil out of the evil storeroom, for his mouth speaks from the overflow of the heart.
—Luke 6:45

Read the passage aloud and listen carefully for the answers to the following questions:

A good man produces what out of the storeroom of his heart?

_____

An evil man produces what out of the storeroom of his heart?

_____

The mouth speaks from the overflow of what?

_____

Bringing It Home

Jessa had always wondered what it would be like to sit at the "cool table" at lunch. She would see the girls whispering and laughing, and it always looked like they were having more fun than everyone else. And then one day, it happened. She had been put in the same group with Bailey, one of the girls in her science class, and before long, they struck up a friendship. At the end of class one day, Bailey said, "Hey, you should sit with us at lunch today." It was good timing because Jessa hadn't really found a group to sit with yet, and she'd been floating from table to table.

Once she had a seat at the cool table, she quickly realized most of their laughter was at the expense of others. Bailey was nice and didn't say much, but her friends made fun of other kids walking by. One of the girls even called one of the teachers a bad name. Jessa knew she didn't fit in at the table and wondered why a sweet girl like Bailey would want to sit with this group. If this was the price to pay in order to be considered "cool," no thanks.

What does God's Word say?

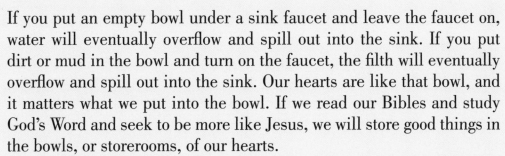

If you put an empty bowl under a sink faucet and leave the faucet on, water will eventually overflow and spill out into the sink. If you put dirt or mud in the bowl and turn on the faucet, the filth will eventually overflow and spill out into the sink. Our hearts are like that bowl, and it matters what we put into the bowl. If we read our Bibles and study God's Word and seek to be more like Jesus, we will store good things in the bowls, or storerooms, of our hearts.

On the other hand, if we fill the storerooms of our hearts with filth, it will eventually come out in the way we speak. Because of sin, we will all say evil things at times, but this passage is warning against filling up the evil storeroom of our hearts and doing nothing to empty it. It's important to know that we can empty the evil from the storeroom by turning to Christ (repenting) and asking for forgiveness.

Think About It

Is there a connection between what comes out of our mouths and what is in our hearts? What is it?

Talk About It

Questions to ask your mom:

If someone were to follow you around for a day and listen to the things you say, would they say the storeroom of your heart is mainly good or evil?

What rules have you made in order to protect my heart from evil influences?

Questions for your mom to ask you:

What are some ways evil can fill up the storeroom of a person's heart?

What are some ways you can build up the good in the store-room of your heart?

_____

_____

_____

_____

_____

_____

This Week

Pay careful attention this week to the things you say. When you are tempted to say something unkind, stop, take a breath, and pray. Ask God to help you speak from the overflow of the good storeroom of your heart.

Keep Going

If you fill the storeroom of your heart with the influences below, how might it affect the words you speak? Write down your answer below each influence.

Songs with bad words

_____

TV shows with violence and bad language

_____

Inappropriate websites

_____

Video games with violent themes

_____

Hanging out with girls who talk badly about others

_____

Reading books with mature (grown-up) themes

_____

Week 18:
Knock, Knock

Bible Reading

"Keep asking, and it will be given to you. Keep searching, and you will find. Keep knocking, and the door will be opened to you. For everyone who asks receives, and the one who searches finds, and to the one who knocks, the door will be opened."

—Matthew 7:7–8

Read the passage aloud and listen carefully for the answers to the following questions:

The passage tells us to keep doing three things. What are they?

_____

_____

_____

Will God open or close the door when we knock?

_____

Bringing It Home

Twenty-three days. That's how many days in a row Peyton prayed and asked God to give her a puppy. Ever since she had spent the night at Grace's house and played with her brand-new puppy, Peyton knew she wanted a dog of her own. When she got home, she begged her parents, but they told her it wasn't a good time. "Maybe next year," they said. Ugh. She hated to wait for things. They were about to start remodeling the kitchen and said it would be too much work to train the puppy and handle the remodel. She begged some more. She pleaded. And they kept saying no. In fact, they threatened to ground her if she asked again, so she knew she better come up with another plan.

That's when she turned to God. She remembered the verses in the Bible that said to "ask and it will be given to you." So, she decided to ask. Every day. For twenty-three days straight she asked God for a puppy. But on day number twenty-four, she began to wonder if God was hearing her prayers. Why would the Bible say that if you asked it would be given to you, if God wasn't planning to deliver on His promise?

What does God's Word say?

God never promised to give us everything we ask for. He hears all our prayers, but He answers our prayers according to His will, not our desires. His reason for telling us to keep asking, keep searching, and keep knocking is to keep us connected to Him. He wants to have a relationship with us, but He wants it to be a two-way street. If we show up with a long list of requests and the focus is on what we want Him to do for us, it is not much of a relationship. The more time we spend with Him, the more likely His desires will become our desires.

Think About It

Have you ever asked God for something? Did you ask according to His will or according to your desires?

Talk About It

Questions to ask your mom:

What is a request you keep making of God? Do you end your request by telling God, "Your will be done"?

_____

_____

_____

_____

_____

_____

What do you do to "keep searching"?

_____

_____

_____

_____

_____

Questions for your mom to ask you:

How will this passage change the way you pray and ask God for things?

_____

_____

_____

_____

_____

What do you do to "keep searching"?

_____

_____

_____

_____

_____

_____

This Week

Practice going to God in prayer and making your requests of Him, but end with "Your will be done."

Keep Going

Pick one of the sentences below and draw a picture to describe it. Have your mom do the same thing, but don't tell each other which one you are picking. When you are finished, see if you can guess which one each other picked.

Keep asking and it will be given to you.

Keep searching and you will find it.

Keep knocking and the door will be opened to you.

Week 19:
Share the Good News!

Bible Reading

Therefore, we are ambassadors for Christ, certain that God is appealing through us. We plead on Christ's behalf, "Be reconciled to God."

—2 Corinthians 5:20

Read the passage aloud, and listen carefully for the answers to the following questions. (Warning: There are some big words in this passage, but we'll talk about them!)

God has given us the ministry of what?

_____

_____

We are ambassadors for whom?

_____

_____

Bringing It Home

Claire thought it was exciting enough that her science project was awarded first prize at Oak Valley Elementary, but when she walked into the fancy hotel ballroom and saw all the winning projects from across the state, it took her breath away. Her principal had made a big deal the day before during the school announcements, telling the student body that Claire would be going to the finalist competition to represent the entire school in the science fair.

Each of the finalists would be given two minutes to explain their projects, and she had practiced what she would say for weeks. She knew it was a huge responsibility, and she wanted to make her school proud. She was nervous, so she said a prayer before it started and asked God to calm her nerves. She looked over her notes one last time before the program started.

What does God's Word say?

Most every person wonders what their purpose in life is. I'm not really talking about your grown-up job, but rather your spiritual job. For Christians, God has given us the job title of "ambassador." An ambassador is "an authorized messenger or representative." We are called to represent Christ, and more importantly, to point others to Him. Maybe you've heard the phrase "the good news" in church before. The good news is the gospel message that Jesus died for the sins of all mankind in order that they might have a relationship with God. God is pure and holy and can't be in the presence of sin, or He would cease to be holy. He sent His Son, Jesus, to die for our sins, and the Bible says we are washed whiter than snow.

As Christ's ambassadors, we have been given the awesome job of telling as many people as possible that God loves them and wants to be reconciled to them. *Reconciled* means to "restore" or "bring back together." If you are a Christian, your sins have been forgiven and you are reconciled to God. That is the good news, but it gets even better! We are also promised eternal life. No wonder God wants us to share that same good news with others. We represent Him, and as a result, we should want to make Him proud.

Think About It

Did you know you were given the job of "ambassador"?

Talk About It

Questions to ask your mom:

Tell me about when you were "reconciled to God."

_____

_____

_____

_____

_____

How do you share the good news with others?

_____

_____

_____

_____

_____

Questions for your mom to ask you:

Do you understand what being reconciled to God means?

_____

_____

_____

_____

_____

How can you be a good ambassador (representative) for Christ?

_____

_____

_____

_____

_____

This Week

Pray and ask God to show you one person who needs to hear the good news; then share it with them.

Keep Going

Pretend you are having a conversation with a good friend and one day she tells you, "I don't really understand what Christians believe. I know you're a Christian, so explain it to me." Since you are an ambassador, you need to be ready to tell her (or whomever) what the good news is. Below, write out what you would say as a response to your friend.

_____

_____

_____

_____

_____

_____

_____

_____

Week 20:
Grrrrrrr

Bible Reading

Do everything without grumbling and arguing, so that you may be blameless and pure, children of God who are faultless in a crooked and perverted generation, among whom you shine like stars in the world.
—Philippians 2:14–15

Read the passage aloud and listen carefully for the answers to the following questions:

Do everything without what?

_____

When we do, we will shine like what?

_____

Bringing It Home

Erin was fuming. "Well, what did your mom say?" asked her friend Ashlyn.

"She said I have to go to my grandparents' house and can't stay later to watch the movie." Erin left out the part where her mother also grounded her from TV when she got home, after arguing and complaining about going to her grandparents' house later that evening for dinner. It had been on the calendar for over a week, but she was going to see her grandparents the next week anyway for her sister's birthday. She didn't see what the big deal was in asking if she could skip the dinner and stay longer at her friend's house.

She had texted her mom about it twice before calling and begging over the phone to get out of the dinner, but that only made her mom more mad. Whenever her mom reached the point of saying, "If I hear one more word about it . . . ," it was a warning sign to stop the complaining. Unfortunately, Erin had kept pushing. And now, she was grounded from TV on top of having to leave her friend's house earlier than she wanted. *Ugh*, Erin thought. *Sometimes life is so unfair.*

What does God's Word say?

God's Word tells us to do everything without grumbling and complaining. Sometimes, when we don't understand the reason behind something, it's hard to keep our mouths shut and resist arguing back. Children of God are supposed to behave differently and show respect to those in authority. When we honor others, we are actually honoring God as well. This is one way we shine like stars in this world.

This doesn't mean you can't respectfully approach someone if you think something they are asking you to do is unfair. There is a big difference between arguing back with someone and making a reasonable appeal. When you make an appeal, you use a calm tone of voice and make the request once. If the person in authority still doesn't give in, you should respectfully do as they ask without complaining or arguing. (Unless they are asking you to do something that is illegal or immoral—and in that case, you should talk to someone you can trust!)

When you are tempted to argue, a good rule of thumb is to take a breath and pray first. Ask God to help you understand the other person's point of view. If you have a bad habit of arguing and complaining, ask God to help you overcome it. You might even try to memorize this week's verse and tuck it away in your heart for a rainy day.

Think About It

Do you have a problem with grumbling and complaining?

Talk About It

Questions to ask your mom:

Do you think I have a problem with grumbling and complaining?

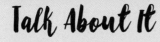

If I practice making an "appeal" instead of grumbling and complaining, how might that sound? (Example: "Mom, I respect your decision, but can I make an appeal?")

_____

_____

_____

_____

Questions for your mom to ask you:

When you are tempted to grumble and complain, what is something I can say to you to help you stop and take a breath (and pray)? Maybe a secret word that we have between ourselves?

_____

_____

_____

_____

Do you think I have a problem with grumbling and complaining?

_____

_____

_____

_____

_____

This Week

Be on the lookout for situations where you are tempted to grumble and complain. Each time, try to catch yourself, take a breath, and pray before responding. Write the situations down in a journal and count them up at the end of the week to see if grumbling and complaining has become a pattern for you.

Keep Going

Take the quiz to see if you're a complainer. Circle your answers.

1. Your dad tells you to fold the laundry, but you are busy video-chatting with a friend. You . . .

    a. say, "Ugh, do I have to do it right now?!"

    b. say, "Yes, sir," and tell your friend you'll call her back when you're done.

2. Your teacher gives the class homework on Friday right before the bell rings. You . . .

    a. storm out of the class and tell your mom when you get in the car that your weekend is ruined.

    b. aren't happy about it, but hey. She's the teacher, and she sets the rules.

3. One of your friends asks if you can spend the night, but your parents don't feel comfortable just yet with you staying over-night somewhere else. You . . .

    a. scream, "Life is so unfair!" You storm up to your room and slam the door.

    b. are disappointed and ask them if they'll think about it, but you will respect whatever they decide.

4. It's your sister's turn to choose the family movie, and she picks one that you don't like. You . . .

   a. announce that you're not watching the stupid movie.

   b. don't say anything. It will be your turn to choose the movie next time, and who knows. You may like this one anyway.

5. You don't get the session of summer camp you were hoping for. You . . .

   a. tell your parents you don't even want to go. All your friends are in a different session, and there's no way it will be any fun.

   b. are disappointed, but you decide to give it a try. Maybe you'll meet some new friends.

How Did You Do?

If you answered mostly *a*, you have a problem with complaining. Ask God to help you break the cycle and respond in a way that would honor God.

If you answered mostly *b*, you're doing great! Congratulations, and keep up with the good work!

Week 21:
Helping Hands

Bible Reading

"What then should we do?" the crowds were asking him. He replied to them, "The one who has two shirts must share with someone who has none, and the one who has food must do the same."

—Luke 3:10–11

Read the passage aloud and listen carefully for the answers to the following questions:

What question did the crowds ask Jesus?

_____

_____

What did Jesus tell them to do?

_____

_____

_____

Bringing It Home

Riley couldn't help but notice the new girl who was sitting at the end of her lunch table. As the girl pulled out a single piece of bread and an apple, she looked up, caught Riley staring in her direction, then looked down again, self-conscious about her sparse lunch. Riley felt bad for watching her, but she wondered why the girl didn't bring more food for lunch. It had been one week since she had started coming to Riley's school, and she had worn the same shirt for three of the five days.

Later that day, the new girl was on Riley's bus and sat on the row behind her. Riley decided to introduce herself, and the girl said her name was Maggie and that she had moved from another state so her family could be closer to relatives while her dad looked for a job. They talked some about school, then Maggie stood up to get off at the next stop—an old, weathered apartment complex. She smiled shyly at Riley as she stepped off the bus. As Riley watched her walk toward the apartments, she realized that Maggie didn't have much in her lunch and had worn the same shirt because her family didn't have much money.

Riley thought about the pile of clothes and shoes her mother had just made her dig through the weekend before to see what no longer fit and could be donated Goodwill. She felt a pang of guilt as the bus pulled into her neighborhood and past tidy two-story brick houses. Most of her friends lived in the same neighborhood, and up until that moment, she had just assumed that most of the kids at her school lived in homes like hers. She guessed they all had closets filled with clothes and pantries stocked with plenty of food too. As she got off the bus, she wondered how she could reach out to Maggie and share some of her things without embarrassing her. Becoming her friend was a good start.

What does God's Word say?

Sometimes it's easy to forget that there are many around us who don't have the same advantages we do. Some kids come home to empty refrigerators and wonder where their next meal will come from. Others may have just enough for food, but they've never had a new outfit that wasn't a hand-me-down from an older sibling. Yet, others are blessed beyond belief and have clothes in their closets and drawers that they've hardly worn. They throw out food that goes bad in their pantries, and sometimes they complain about the things their moms pack in their lunches.

God's Word tells us to look out for the poor, but many of us don't know where to start. Christians have a responsibility to help the poor and the needy, yet many have turned a blind eye to the needs around them.

Loving those who are less fortunate goes beyond telling them about Jesus. Many of them know Jesus already and are "needy" in a different way. If we are to help the poor and needy, it begins by opening our eyes to their needs and asking God how we can help. We must be willing to see the problem and become a part of the solution.

Think About It

Do you think much about helping the poor and needy?

Talk About It

Questions to ask your mom:

What are some ways our family reaches out to the poor and needy?

_____

_____

_____

_____

Do you think we could do more to help?

_____

_____

_____

Questions for your mom to ask you:

Who are you more like in the Bible verse: the one who has two shirts, or the one who has none?

_____

_____

_____

When you think about the clothes in your drawers and closet and the food in our pantry, in what ways are we guilty of being wasteful?

_____

_____

_____

_____

_____

What are some ways we can do a better job of sharing what we have with the poor and needy?

_____

_____

_____

_____

_____

_____

This Week

Find some time this week to go through your closet and drawers and make a pile of things that no longer fit or that you no longer wear. Ask your mom to help you find a place to donate your extra clothes.

Keep Going

Look at the list below, and choose one or two ways you can help the needy this next week.

____ Buy extra food at the grocery store the next time you go shopping and drop it off at a nearby food pantry.

____ Volunteer to serve food to the homeless or work in a soup kitchen.

____ Go through your closet, bag up the clothes and shoes you no longer wear, and donate them.

____ Sponsor a child or family during the Christmas holidays and find out what they need. Take up an offering or go shopping for them.

_____ Ask your mom and dad if you can buy granola bars and bottled water to keep in the car and hand out to the homeless people you see in your community.

_____ Ask your parents if your family can volunteer to do a mission project over the summer.

_____ Use some of your allowance to help sponsor a needy child in another country through Compassion, World Vision, or a similar type of organization.

_____ Go through your old books and toys, and donate them to a shelter.

Week 22:
Pinky Swear Promise

Bible Reading

Now above all, my brothers, do not swear, either by heaven or by earth or with any other oath. Your "yes" must be "yes," and your "no" must be "no," so that you won't fall under judgment.

— James 5:12

Read the passage aloud, and listen carefully for the answers to the following questions:

What does the passage say we should not do?

_____

Your "yes" must be what? And your "no" must be what?

_____

Bringing It Home

"Are you going to save me a seat on the bus for the field trip if your class gets on first?" Emma Kate asked her friend Keely on the way to school. "Yes, I swear," Keely said. "Pinky swear?" asked Emma Kate. "Sure, whatever!" said Keely. "I swear on a stack of Bibles that I'll save you a seat." Emma Kate could hardly wait for the field trip to the zoo. They would be gone for most of the day, and she couldn't wait to ride the bus and hang out with her friends. Any day that didn't include math was guaranteed to be a good day.

Finally the morning bell rang, and her teacher had them line up to get on the bus. Keely's class was already on the bus, and Emma Kate saw Keely through the window as she lined up single file with her class. _Wait, it looks like someone is next to her!_ thought Emma Kate. Sure enough when she boarded the bus, she saw Keely looking right at her and shrugging as she mouthed, "I'm sorry." As she took a seat toward the front of the bus, Emma Kate was fuming. Keely had a bad habit of giving her word and then not keeping it. It was getting harder and harder to trust her. Maybe it was time to find a new friend.

What does God's Word say?

Swearing on the Bible or to God may not seem like a big deal, but it is a big deal to God. God wants us to mean what we say and say what we mean. There is no need to swear because all that is required is a simple yes or a simple no. That is what it means in the passage when it says, "Your 'yes' must be 'yes,' and your 'no' must be 'no.'" It's important to tell the truth, so we shouldn't have to "swear" to convince someone that we are being honest. When we don't follow through on our word, it will be hard for others to trust that our word means anything in the future. When we swear on the Bible or to God and don't follow through on our promise, we are not just breaking the promise to the person we made it to—we are also breaking the promise to God.

Think About It

Before you read the Bible passage, did you think it was wrong to swear on the Bible or to God?

Talk About It

Questions to ask your mom:

When you were my age, did you ever have a bad habit of swearing on the Bible or to God?

_____

_____

_____

_____

_____

Does your "yes" usually mean "yes" and your "no" mean "no"?

_____

_____

_____

_____

Questions for your mom to ask you:

Do you or any of your friends swear on the Bible or to God?

_____

_____

_____

_____

After reading the passage, do you think it's wrong to swear? What might you say when one of your friends asks you to swear on the Bible or to God?

_____

_____

_____

_____

_____

_____

This Week

Pay attention when someone asks you something and you give them a yes or a no. Did you follow through on your word?

Keep Going

Read the verses below:

"Again, you have heard that it was said to our ancestors, You must not break your oath, but you must keep your oaths to the Lord. But I tell you, don't take an oath at all: either by heaven, because it is God's throne; or by the earth, because it is His footstool; or by Jerusalem, because it is the city of the great King. Neither should you swear by your head, because you cannot make a single hair white or black. But let your word 'yes' be 'yes,' and your 'no' be 'no.' Anything more than this is from the evil one." (Matthew 5:33–37)

Make a list of all the things the verses say not to do:

Week 23:
Above All Else

Bible Reading

Guard your heart above all else,
for it is the source of life.

—Proverbs 4:23

Read the passage aloud and listen carefully for the answers to the following questions:

What should we guard above all else?

_____

The heart is the source of what?

_____

Bringing It Home

Ragan looked at the list of daily reminders her dad had taped on her bathroom mirror and felt a twinge of sadness as she read the list.

Brush your teeth

Wash your hands often

Take your vitamins

Exercise

Say your prayers

Guard your heart

Her dad had taught her the importance of taking care of herself so she would be healthy in the years to come. At the time, she didn't really understand what the big deal was about "guarding her heart." I mean, how does someone guard her heart, anyway? Her dad had explained that it was important to care for her heart by protecting it from bad influences that could affect her in the years to come. Now she understood what he was talking about.

Ragan was at lunch with her friends when they started talking about a book they were all reading. It was a book series that all of Ragan's friends were allowed to read, but Ragan's parents didn't think it was "appropriate for girls her age." Ugh. She had been so mad when they told her that. As her friends began to share about the stuff that was happening in the books, she realized why her parents had told her she couldn't read them. She could hardly believe what she was hearing. One of her friends even said, "If my mom knew this was in the book, there's no way she'd let me read them."

Sure, it was frustrating at times to be the only one who wasn't allowed to do some of the things her friends did, but now Ragan understood that her parents were just trying to help her guard her heart.

What does God's Word say?

God's Word tells us to guard our hearts because they are the "source of life." Much like a "source" can be the beginning place of a river or stream, our hearts are the beginning place where the streams of our lives flow. If we pollute the source, it can flow into other areas of our lives further downstream—even if we don't notice it right away.

We guard our hearts by paying careful attention to what we put in them. Most importantly, we fill our hearts with good and godly influences in an effort to guard and protect them from being polluted with the toxic

things of the world. One of the best compliments you could ever receive is, "You have such a good heart." Good hearts don't happen by magic. It takes hard work and diligence to guard and protect them. A guarded heart is a good heart.

Think About It

Would you like to hear someone say that you have a "good heart"?

Talk About It

Questions to ask your mom:

When you were my age, did you work hard at "guarding your heart"?

_____

_____

What are some things you do today to "guard your heart" from things that might pollute your life?

_____

_____

_____

Questions for your mom to ask you:

Is it hard for you sometimes to understand why we have certain rules in place to help guard and protect your heart?

_____

_____

_____

Can you think of someone you know who has a good heart?
What about them makes you think that?

_____

_____

_____

This Week

As you go through the week, pay careful attention to situations you find yourself in where you are faced with a choice to either guard your heart or give in to something that might not be good for your heart. Make a list below to share with your mother next week. Have her do the same thing.

_____

_____

_____

_____

Keep Going

Write out Proverbs 4:23 (or print it out) and post it someplace (on your bathroom mirror, in your locker, on your school folder, etc.) where you will be reminded to guard your heart.

Close your eyes and draw a picture below of a "guarded heart." (This is just for fun, so be creative!) Now, have your mom try it too. Which picture is the best?

Week 24:
A New Pendant

Bible Reading

Listen, my son, to your father's instruction, and don't reject your mother's teaching, for they will be a garland of grace on your head and a gold chain around your neck.

—Proverbs 1:8–9

179

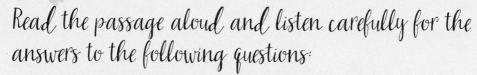

Read the passage aloud and listen carefully for the answers to the following questions:

Children should listen to their father's what?

_____

And they should not reject their mother's what?

_____

Bringing It Home

Nora looked down at the crack in the corner of her dad's tablet in disbelief. She had gone to grab the throw blanket on the couch, and the tablet must have been tucked between the folds. When she had yanked the blanket, the tablet had flown across the room and onto the tile floor.

She said a silent prayer as she pushed the home button to see if it would still turn on. Fortunately, it did, but there was no hiding the crackled screen in the top corner. Her parents had just started letting her use their tablet when they weren't using it, and they had given her specific instructions to always put it back on the desk in the office when she was finished. Just last week, her dad had sat down with her and explained how she was getting older and could be trusted with more responsibility. And now, this.

Nora knew she would have to tell her parents when they got home. She had no choice but to be honest with them and tell them she was sorry. She knew there might be consequences for not listening to her parents and putting the tablet back where it belonged, but she knew her parents would forgive her and give her another chance.

What does God's Word say?

Sometimes we don't understand why our parents have so many rules, or why they spend so much time trying to teach us how to be responsible. God's Word reminds us of the importance of not just respecting our parents, but also of listening to their instruction and teaching. He likens their teaching and instruction to a "garland of grace" and a "gold chain." Many of us think of garland as something we use to decorate at Christmastime. Maybe your mom drapes garland along the stairway railing or on the fireplace. Or maybe you hang strands of garland on your Christmas tree. Just as a garland makes an ordinary object look better, our parents' instruction and teaching makes us better people. It is like a gold necklace because it is of great worth and value. The next time you feel an urge to grumble or complain about your parents' instruction or teaching, remember that truth!

Think About It

Do you think of your parents' teaching and instruction as something valuable?

Talk About It

Questions to ask your mom:

Did you appreciate your parents' teaching and instruction when you were my age? Why or why not?

_____

_____

_____

_____

Can you think of a time when you didn't follow their teaching or instruction? What happened?

_____

_____

_____

_____

Questions for your mom to ask you:

When it comes to our rules, are there any that are frustrating to you? Why?

Why do you think it's important to follow our teaching and instruction?

This Week

This week, when your parents give you instruction or teaching, do your best to follow it without grumbling or complaining. As a bonus, thank them for taking the time to make you a better person.

Keep Going

Think of three rules your parents have, and list them below. After each one, write down why you think your parents have the rule and what they are trying to teach you.

1.

Why:

_____

_____

_____

2.

Why:

_____

_____

_____

3.

Why:

_____

_____

_____

Week 25:
Clean Slate

Bible Reading

If we confess our sins, He is faithful and righteous to forgive us our sins and to cleanse us from all unrighteousness.

—1 John 1:9

Read the passage aloud and listen carefully for the answers to the following questions:

If we confess our sins, God is faithful and righteous to do what?

_____

God will cleanse us from what?

_____

Bringing It Home

Elizabeth couldn't sleep. The secret was killing her. Earlier in the day, she had let the dog out of its crate because it was whimpering and driving her crazy. Her parents didn't mind if she opened the crate as long as she took the dog outside right away to go to the bathroom. At the time, she was trying to watch her favorite show and meant to take the dog out when the show ended. But yep, she forgot—and the dog went to the bathroom on the kitchen floor. As if that wasn't bad enough, her mom stepped in it when she got home from work.

Rather than tell her mom the truth, Elizabeth had blamed it on her little brother. He was a toddler and had just learned to unlatch the door to the crate, so her mother would never suspect that he didn't do it. She would just assume the babysitter wasn't watching when he let the dog out. And Elizabeth was right; her mom fell for the lie.

But now Elizabeth couldn't sleep because the guilt was nagging at her. She didn't even want to say her bedtime prayers because she felt distant from God after telling the lie. She knew she needed to tell her mother the truth, but first she would confess it to God. Even though she felt distant, she knew God would forgive her. And her mother would forgive her too, even if she did ground her. *Funny,* she thought. *Being grounded would not be nearly as bad as hiding the sin and living with the lie.*

What does God's Word say?

God knows we are sinners and that even after we become Christians, we will still commit sins. No sin is too big for God to forgive. He wants us to *confess* when we sin (admit what we did), and turn to Him for forgiveness. God is always faithful to forgive us and help us start over.

It's like one of those Etch A Sketch toys: You turn the knobs to make a picture or design, then shake it to make it all disappear. When we confess our sins, God removes them and gives us grace (forgiveness) in their place. In fact, when He looks at us, He doesn't see the sin at all! We're like a blank Etch A Sketch. A clean slate.

Think About It

Have you ever hidden a sin and not confessed it? How did it make you feel?

Talk About It

Questions to ask your mom:

When you were growing up, did you confess your sins to God when you did something wrong?

_____

_____

_____

_____

Can you think of a time when you tried to live with a sin and didn't confess it? Did you feel guilty?

_____

_____

_____

_____

Is it hard for you to believe God has really forgiven everything you've ever done?

Questions for your mom to ask you:

Do you confess your sins to God when you do things that are wrong?

Is it hard for you to confess to your father or me? If yes, why is that?

_____

_____

_____

_____

_____

This Week

Each night before you go to bed, spend some time praying and confessing your sins to God. Try to think through your day and ask Him to show you sins that might need to be confessed. Thank Him for His forgiveness.

Keep Going

Our sins are like stains on our hearts, but when we confess them to God, He cleanses (removes) them and makes us clean again. Unscramble the words to find out what cleanses each of the items below:

A dirty car: __ __ __   __ __ __ __
r c a   s w h a

A stain on your shirt: __ __ __ __ __ __ __   __ __ __ __ __ __ __ __ __
t s c o e l h   g n e t t e r e d

Germs on your hands: __ __ __ __   __ __ __ __ __ __ __ __ __
a h d n   e s t a i z r i n

Dirty dishes: __ __ __ __   __ __ __ __
i d h s   p o s a

A smudged windshield: __ __ __ __ __ __ __ __ __   __ __ __ __ __
s i d l w e n i d h   i r p e w

Week 26:
A Day to Remember

Bible Reading

Remember the Sabbath day, to keep it holy. You are to labor six days and do all your work, but the seventh day is a Sabbath to the LORD your God.
—Exodus 20:8-10

Read the passage aloud and listen carefully for the answers to the following questions:

What are we supposed to remember and keep holy?

_____

The Sabbath is for the sake of remembering whom?

_____

Bringing It Home

Macy could hardly wait to share the good news with her mom after her cheer class. Tryouts for the competitive cheer team were next week, and her coach had pulled her aside and encouraged her to try out for the team. One of her friends was on the team last year and got to travel to different cities for the competitions on the weekends. She came home with trophies, jackets, and ribbons, which were on proud display in her room. Macy had tried different sports and activities in the past, but didn't stay interested for long. Until cheerleading. She had finally found her thing.

When her friend's mom dropped Macy off at home, she rushed in the door and shared the good news with her parents. When excited, she tended to talk too fast, so her dad said, "Slow down! We can't understand what you're saying!" She took a breath and told them the news. When she finished, her parents were silent for a minute, and she wondered why they weren't excited for her. Then her mom spoke up. "Honey, that is wonderful that your coach thinks you have what it takes to be on the competitive team. Unfortunately, competitive cheer costs a lot of money, and even if we were to be able to work it into the budget, the competitions are on the weekends—which means you would have to miss church quite a bit."

"Mom, it's not that big of a deal! All my friends do stuff on the weekends and miss church!"

Macy's mom agreed to call her coach and get more information about the weekend travel requirements. But Macy knew that if being on the team meant missing church a lot, her parents would choose church over competitive cheer. *Ugh*, thought Macy. Why was it so hard to be a Christian sometimes?

What does God's Word say?

Macy is right. It is hard to be a Christian. It requires commitment, and sometimes commitment requires that we give things up that get in the way of our faith. When God set apart a day for the Sabbath, He did it so we would have a day to pause and take a break to remember Him. He modeled Sabbath rest when He created the world and on the seventh day, He rested from all He had done (Genesis 2:2). It's important to note that God did not rest because He was tired. God doesn't need to rest. He rested because He wanted to set an example for us to have a day when we cease from our work and remember Him.

Christians today are not as faithful when it comes to setting aside a day for rest and reflection. Church is not mandatory as a Christian, but it is very important. The Bible also talks about the "fellowship" of believers and the importance of gathering together with others who believe in Christ and follow Him (Acts 2:42). Some families attend a church with Saturday services if they aren't able to commit to Sabbath rest on Sunday or devote another day to resting and gathering together with

other believers. We need to be careful that we don't allow other things to become more important than our faith. Look at it this way: God has graciously given us all our days. Is it too much to ask that we set aside one day each week just for Him?

Think About It

After reading the verses above, do you think it's important to set aside one day a week to rest and gather with other believers to remember God?

Talk About It

Questions to ask your mom:

What do you do to practice Sabbath rest?

_____

_____

_____

_____

_____

Do you think it's important for our family to have a church home and be involved? Why or why not?

_____

_____

_____

_____

_____

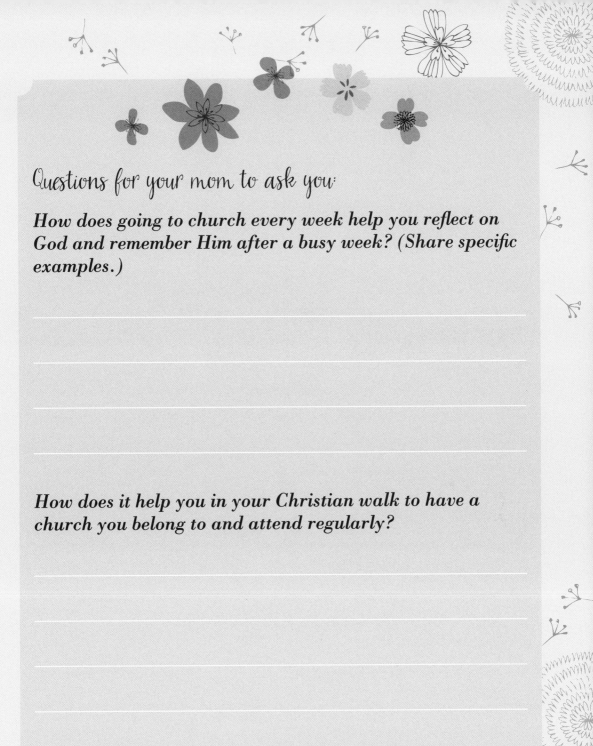

Questions for your mom to ask you:

How does going to church every week help you reflect on God and remember Him after a busy week? (Share specific examples.)

_____

_____

_____

_____

How does it help you in your Christian walk to have a church you belong to and attend regularly?

_____

_____

_____

_____

This Week

If you don't have a church you belong to (or visit on a regular basis), ask around and find a church to attend this Sunday. If you've been visiting a church, what is holding you back from joining? If it's not the right fit for your family, begin visiting other churches this Sunday. Make it your goal to find a church you can call home.

Keep Going

True or False?

To encourage people to reserve Sundays as a day for rest and religious activities:

1. Many stores used to be closed on Sunday to encourage participation in religious activities.   True   False

2. In some states, the sale of alcohol is forbidden on Sundays.   True   False

3. It used to be unheard of for team sports (practices or games) to be held on Sundays.   True   False

4. Hunting used to be banned on Sundays.   True   False

5. In many states, you cannot buy a car on Sundays.   True   False

ANSWERS: They are all true!

Week 27:
Weekend Friends

Bible Reading

Do not be deceived: "Bad company corrupts good morals."
—1 Corinthians 15:33

Read the passage aloud and listen carefully for the answers to the following questions:

Do not be what?

_____

What corrupts good morals?

_____

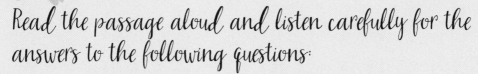

Bringing It Home

There was no telling how long Jessica would be grounded from TV and the computer. Her mom had been getting onto her a lot lately for her attitude. This time Jessica had gone too far. One of her friends had called to see if she could go to a movie in about an hour. Her mom told her she could if she got all her chores done. She had been putting them off all week, and now, there was no way she could get them done in time.

In her frustration Jessica snapped back. "Ugh! You are so annoying sometimes! Most of my friends don't even have to do stupid chores!" And yeah, she'd been in her room ever since. Her mom had come in to talk, and she said she was concerned about the new group of girls Jessica was hanging out with. She had noticed that many of them had really bad attitudes and wondered if maybe that's why Jessica was losing her temper more easily and talking back more often. It made

Jessica mad that her mom brought it up, but as she thought about it more, she realized it was true that her attitude had gotten really bad since she started hanging out with this group of girls.

What does God's Word say?

Maybe you've heard the saying, "You are who you hang out with." If you spend a lot of time with certain people, after a while, some of their habits may rub off on you. That's why it's important to choose our friends wisely. If we choose friends who have bad habits, we may find ourselves eventually adopting the same bad habits.

When my daughter was your age, I talked to her about "weekday friends" and "weekend friends." I told her that many of the girls she meets won't share the same morals and values that she has, and they would make good weekday friends. Weekday friends are friends you see at school, sit with at lunch, or hang out with at times, at your house.

Weekend friends are friends who share the same values, morals, and beliefs that you have. They are the friends your mom and dad are okay with you spending time with on the weekends, and maybe even spending the night (at your house or theirs). Their parents have the same values and rules, so you know you won't be in difficult situations where you face temptations to do things that would compromise your faith. You might not have as many weekend friends as you do weekday friends because weekend friends are special.

If you are choosy about the kinds of friends you spend time with, your morals are not as likely to be "corrupted by bad company."

Think About It

Have you noticed that spending a lot of time with someone can cause you to be more like that person?

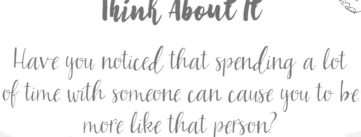

Talk About It

Questions to ask your mom:

Can you think of a time when you were growing up that "bad company corrupted good morals"? What happened?

_____

_____

_____

_____

_____

Why is it still important even at your age to be picky about the kind of friends you have?

_____

_____

_____

_____

Questions for your mom to ask you:

Can you think of an example of when "bad company corrupted good morals"? (Maybe you know someone who found new friends, and you noticed their behavior begin to change.)

_____

_____

_____

_____

This Week

Spend some time thinking about the friends you have now. No one is perfect (neither are you!), but pray and ask God to show you if you need to spend less time with any of your friends whose company might corrupt your good morals. Also, ask God to show you if you are being a bad influence or a good influence on others.

Keep Going

Look back at the definitions of "weekday friends" and "weekend friends." Write down names of your current friends in each category. Also, be open to new friends who might make good weekend friends. You might even get your mom to help you on this one! (Note: Do not share this list with anyone other than your mom or dad, and don't talk about it with your friends. It could be hurtful if one of your friends discovered they were on your "weekday friends" list.)

Weekday Friends

Weekend Friends

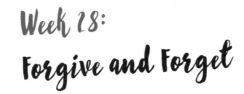

Week 28:
Forgive and Forget

Bible Reading

Put on heartfelt compassion, kindness, humility, gentleness, and patience, accepting one another and forgiving one another if anyone has a complaint against another. Just as the Lord has forgiven you, so you must also forgive.

—Colossians 3:12-13

Read the passage aloud and listen carefully for the answers to the following questions:

God calls us to be accepting and forgiving of whom?

_____

Why is it important to forgive others?

_____

_____

_____

Bringing It Home

Sophie's mom had tried to warn her about Kenzie, but Sophie hadn't listened. Kenzie had a bad habit of not keeping her word. This time, Kenzie had gone too far. All year, they had talked about going to the same summer camp session and planned to request the same cabin. Sophie had been going to the same session for years, but Kenzie's family vacation was the same week, so Sophie agreed to switch sessions so they could be together.

Sophie had just received her cabin assignment and called Kenzie immediately to see if they had gotten into the same cabin. She was going to be sad if they didn't, but at least they would be at camp together during the same session. The girls' cabins did most all of the recreation activities together, so they would still be able to see each other. When

Kenzie answered the phone, Sophie was so excited that she practically screamed. "I got my cabin assignment for camp today! Did you get yours?! Hurry, tell your mom to check her e-mail now!" Dead silence. "Kenzie, are you there?"

"Uh, yeah. I forgot to tell you that I changed my mind about going to summer camp. My mom never registered me."

Sophie could hardly believe what she was hearing. She had changed from her regular session just for Kenzie, and now Kenzie wasn't even going! And Kenzie had known it all along, but didn't tell her. Sophie was so upset she didn't know what to say, so she hung up. She wasn't sure she could ever forgive Kenzie for backing out and not telling her. What kind of friend does that?

What does God's Word say?

Forgiveness isn't always easy, but God tells us to forgive just as He has forgiven us. We aren't deserving of His forgiveness, but He sent His Son to die for us anyway. God could have lost patience with us, but He chose to forgive. God could have been angry over our continual sin, but He chose to forgive. God could have turned His back on us, but He chose to forgive. If God can put on compassion, kindness, humility, gentleness, and patience, so can we.

However, forgiveness doesn't always mean trusting someone who hurt you and continuing the friendship. God calls us to treat the other person with compassion, kindness, humility, gentleness, and patience, but in situations where trust is lost, it's a good idea to take a step back from the friendship and allow the other person to earn your trust back.

Think About It

Is it hard for you to forgive
when someone hurts you?

Talk About It

Questions for you to ask your mom:

**When you were my age, do you remember a time when you
had a hard time forgiving someone? What happened?**

Can you think of a time when someone hurt you and it was hard for you to forgive them? What happened?

_____

_____

_____

_____

_____

This Week

Begin a new habit. When you do something wrong and owe someone an apology, don't simply say, "I'm sorry." Follow the apology with a request for forgiveness, as well. "Will you forgive me for _____?"

Keep Going

Draw a line to match the following words with the right definitions. (Use a dictionary if you're not familiar with the meaning of some of the words.)

Compassion   Not thinking too highly of yourself. Thinking of others first.

Kindness   Not severe or rough.

Humility   A feeling of sorrow for someone going through a tough time and a desire to help them through it.

Gentleness   Quiet and steady. Not complaining or losing your temper.

Patience   Being friendly or nice, either by your actions or your words.

Week 29:
Loving the Unlovable

Bible Reading

If your enemy is hungry, give him
food to eat, and if he is thirsty,
give him water to drink; for you will
heap burning coals on his head, and the
LORD will reward you.
—Proverbs 25:21-22

214

Read the passage aloud and listen carefully for the answers to the following questions:

If our enemy is hungry or thirsty, what should we do?

_____

_____

What will God do?

_____

_____

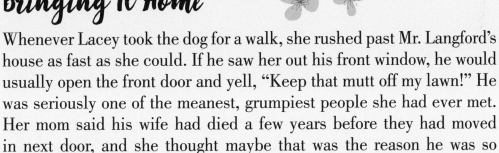

Bringing It Home

Whenever Lacey took the dog for a walk, she rushed past Mr. Langford's house as fast as she could. If he saw her out his front window, he would usually open the front door and yell, "Keep that mutt off my lawn!" He was seriously one of the meanest, grumpiest people she had ever met. Her mom said his wife had died a few years before they had moved in next door, and she thought maybe that was the reason he was so grumpy. Whatever it was, Lacey tried to stay out of his way just to be on the safe side. Sometimes her mom included Mr. Langford when they were saying prayers at bedtime.

That's why she was terrified when her mother asked her one afternoon to come with her to Mr. Langford's house to drop off a letter for him that had mistakenly been left in their mailbox. "Mom, are you serious?

Can't we just toss it over the fence, or leave it on the front porch and ring the doorbell and run away?!" Her mother didn't think her ideas were the least bit amusing. Instead, she suggested they put some of the chocolate chip cookies she had made earlier that day on a plate and give them to Mr. Langford with his mail. *Oh boy*, thought Lacey. *I can't wait to see how this turns out.*

She was pretty sure her teeth were chattering with fear when they rang the doorbell for a second time. When she heard footsteps on the other side of the door and it began to open, she thought she might faint. Before her mother could say a word, Mr. Langford snapped, "Didn't you see the sign? No solicitors!" Her mom, as calm as could be, replied, "Hi, Mr. Langford. We're not solicitors. We live next door, and this letter for you came to our house by mistake." His face was expressionless as he reached out for the letter. "Oh, and we brought you some cookies I made earlier today. I hope you enjoy them." His face softened, and he hesitantly reached out for the plate before mumbling a faint, "Thank you, ma'am." Lacey's mom wished him a good day, and he gently closed the door. As Lacey and her mom made their way back home, her mom reminded her that God calls us to love even the most unlovable people.

The next day when Lacey was walking the dog, Mr. Langford opened his front door. She picked up her pace before he started yelling. Only he didn't yell this time. He walked up the front walk and handed her the plate the cookies had been on. "Tell your mother thank you for me again, please. The cookies were wonderful, and it was very kind of her to think of me. My wife used to make cookies like that, and your mom's cookies were almost as good as hers." Lacey smiled at Mr. Langford and said she would deliver the message. Maybe her mom could make extra cookies for Mr. Langford whenever she baked them. He wasn't that terrifying after all.

What does God's Word say?

The easiest thing to do when we encounter an *enemy* (or someone who is "against us") is to treat them the same way they treat us. Yet, God calls Christians to treat them kindly so that they might see that we are different. Only with the power of Christ living in our hearts are we able to do this. When we respond in a way that is unexpected, it is like "heaping burning coals on their heads." It catches them off guard because they don't expect kindness in return.

As much as we might want to get back at someone who is mean, rude, or unkind, we need to remember that Jesus set the example for how we are to treat our enemies. He was mocked, teased, beaten, and spit upon, and yet when He was nailed to the cross He cried out to God, "Father, forgive them" (Luke 23:34). Jesus could have easily demanded they be punished and condemned to die, but instead, He chose to forgive them. The next time you find yourself wanting to retaliate or get back at someone who has behaved like an enemy, think of Jesus.

Think About It

Is it hard for you to show love to your enemies?

Talk About It

Questions to ask your mom:

Have you ever had an enemy who was hard to love?

_____

_____

_____

_____

How did you show him or her love?

_____

_____

_____

_____

Questions for your mom to ask you:

Can you think of someone at school or church who is hard to love?

_____

_____

_____

_____

How might you show that person love in the week to come?

_____

_____

_____

_____

_____

This Week

Think of something nice to do for the person you mentioned above. Don't forget to pray for him or her on a regular basis!

Keep Going

Circle the response God would want you to have toward an enemy.

1. A mean girl at your school walks by, and just as you are opening your locker, she bumps into it and slams it shut. You . . .

    a. snap back, "Hey, watch where you're going! Do you need glasses or something?!"

    b. say, "You seem like you're having a bad day. Anything I can do to help?"

2. Your soccer team loses to a team that broke a lot of rules during the game by pushing, shoving, and taunting the players on your team. After the game, you . . .

    a. walk by where they are huddled up and loudly say, "The win doesn't count if you had to cheat to get it!"

    b. walk up to their huddle and say, "Good game. Congratulations on the win!"

3. Your neighbor's dog barks all the time, and the neighbor is rude when your parents politely complain. You see him outside one day and . . .

    a. give him a mean look and walk back inside.

    b. say hi and stop to pet his dog.

ANSWERS: 1. B; 2. B; 3. B.

Week 30:
Do-Over

Bible Reading

Therefore, if anyone is in Christ, he is a new creation; old things have passed away, and look, new things have come.

—2 Corinthians 5:17

Read the passage aloud and listen carefully for the answers to the following questions:

If anyone is in Christ, he is what?

_____

What has passed away?

_____

Bringing It Home

Savannah hardly recognized Uncle Mike when she saw him at the family reunion picnic. He had been a no-show the year before, and the year before that, well . . . let's just say he'd had a little too much to drink. He was loud and rude and obnoxious, and all Savannah remembered about that day was that he made her grandmother cry. It was hard to love someone who made sweet Grammy sad. Her mother later told her that Uncle Mike had a drinking problem, and the family hoped he would get some help. Most importantly, she suggested that they begin to pray for him at bedtime. Savannah loved Uncle Mike and had great memories of him playing with all the cousins in years past. He would swing them around in the yard until they were so dizzy they couldn't walk. It made her sad to see that he was not the fun Uncle Mike she had remembered.

When her mom told her that Uncle Mike was going to be at the reunion and that he had changed, she was hesitant to believe it. Looking at him, he certainly looked different. His hair was combed neatly and his face was clean-shaven, which was a huge improvement over the slobbish look he'd had two years ago. Before lunch was served, her dad suggested someone say grace, and Uncle Mike volunteered to pray. That's when Savannah really knew he had changed. He choked back tears as he thanked God for rescuing him from his old life and giving him a new beginning. Savannah couldn't help but glance over at her Grammy during the prayer, who was wiping tears from her eyes. Uncle Mike was back, and they had God to thank for it.

What does God's Word say?

Have you ever needed a "do-over"? Maybe you made a bad grade on a test and wished you could go back and study more and try again. Or maybe you used a sarcastic and disrespectful tone of voice toward your mom or dad and you wished you could go back and unsay it. God's Word tells us that those in Christ (who believe in Him) get a do-over. That doesn't mean they can really go back and undo the bad things they've done, but it promises a fresh start to anyone who needs one. Someone your age may not need a fresh start, but as you get older, you will understand how valuable it is to have a do-over that promises a new and improved life in Christ. The only condition is that we must turn to Him and admit our need for Him. We must tell Him we want to change and become a better person. Part of being a Christ-follower is following His ways and seeking to be more like Him in everything we do. Only Christ has the power to change a life, and His Word assures us that it is never too late to begin again.

Think About It

Do you know someone who could use
a fresh start?

Talk About It

Questions to ask your mom:

What does 2 Corinthians 5:17 mean to you personally?

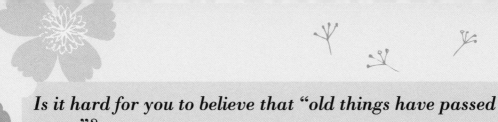

Is it hard for you to believe that "old things have passed away"?

_____

_____

_____

_____

Questions for your mom to ask you:

When you think of a do-over, what are some areas of your life where you wish you could have one?

_____

_____

_____

_____

Becoming a "new creation" doesn't just offer hope for people who have done really terrible things in the past. It's for everyone (because we all have sinned!). In what ways has Christ helped you become a "new creation"? If you are not a Christian, how would a do-over change your life?

This Week

Pay attention this week to areas of your life that may not be pleasing to God. List them in your journal and ask God to help you put those things in your past. Write 2 Corinthians 5:17 at the top of the page and try to memorize it this week.

Keep Going

Look at the situations below. Under each one, write down how being in Christ could help someone become a new creation.

1. Nora gossips all the time. If her mouth is open, chances are she is saying something about someone in a way that isn't very Christlike. How can Christ help Nora become a new creation?

_____

_____

2. Ian is the meanest boy you know. Everyday at recess, he finds someone to pick on and embarrass. Last week he picked up a pile of freshly mowed grass, walked by some girls, and pretended to trip and toss it in their hair. He is desperate for attention, even if it's the wrong kind of attention. How can Christ help Ian become a new creation?

_____

_____

3. Some of your friends have had some things stolen from their lockers. The principal finds out it's a girl in your class who comes from a bad family situation. She has to give everything back and stay after school for a week. How can Christ help her become a new creation?

_____

Week 31:
Beauty That Lasts

Bible Reading

Charm is deceptive and beauty is fleeting, but a woman who fears the LORD will be praised.

—Proverbs 31:30

Read the passage aloud and listen carefully for the answers to the following questions:

What is deceptive?

_____

What is fleeting?

_____

Bringing It Home

Taryn didn't know how much more she could take. Her best friend Amber was getting more and more obnoxious every day. Ever since one of the guys had texted her and told her all the guys thought she was pretty, she had turned into a big flirt. She loved getting their attention and would walk by their group in the morning where they hung out and flip her hair and give them a flirty smile. If she was with the girls and one of the guys walked up, she would totally ignore the girls and start talking to the guys. No matter what the guys said, she laughed and tried to act like she was part of their group.

What's worse, she even started dressing differently and wearing makeup to get the guys' attention. She obsessed over what they thought about her and did whatever it took to be the "pretty girl." If Taryn mentioned having a crush on a certain guy, Amber seemed to go out of her way to get that guy to notice _her_. The guys all seemed to love it, but Taryn and her friends were tired of always taking second place to the guys. Maybe it was time to have a little talk with her . . . if she would listen!

What does God's Word say?

If you look up *charm* in the dictionary, it is defined as "a power of pleasing or attracting, as through personality or beauty." While it might sound like a good quality to have, the Bible warns against it if it is used to attract the opposite sex. For example, it's a good thing if someone compliments you and says, "She's such a charming girl." Charm in that instance refers to kindness and overall likability. The kind of charm the Bible warns against and calls "deceptive" is a flirty type of charm. *Deceptive* means "misleading" or even "dishonest." It is not a kindness extended to others, but rather a means to get others to notice the "charmer."

The Bible also warns that beauty is "fleeting." *Fleeting* means "passing" or "vanishing quickly." Even the prettiest of girls won't stay pretty forever. That is why the Bible warns us against relying on beauty to feel good about ourselves. Outer beauty fades over time, but inner beauty will last forever. A woman who "fears the Lord" is worthy of praise because she focuses on God rather than herself. To "fear the Lord" is not to be afraid of God, but to be in awe of Him and respect Him. The world is filled with girls and women who want nothing more than to be pretty and charming, but few will be truly beautiful women who love and fear the Lord.

Think About It

Would you rather be known as the pretty girl or a girl who loves and fears the Lord?

Talk About It

Questions to ask your mom:

When you were my age, was there a girl in your school who was known as charming or pretty?

_____

_____

_____

_____

What have you noticed about women your age who relied too much on charm and outer appearance? (Did it make them happy?)

_____

_____

_____

_____

Questions for your mom to ask you:

Are there girls in your school who rely on charm and beauty to get the guys to notice them? Why do you think they do that?

_____

_____

_____

_____

What are some ways you can become a young woman who fears the Lord?

_____

_____

_____

_____

This Week

Pay attention to how often you hear someone refer to outer beauty or charm. Maybe it's an ad you see on TV or a comment made about how someone looks. Every time you hear a comment about outer beauty or charm, write it down in your journal. At the end of the week, take a look at how many times you heard comments related to outer beauty. Do you think our culture is more focused on outer beauty or inner beauty?

Keep Going

Label each of the examples below with the quality that matches them, using this key:

(A) = A fear of the Lord

(B) = Beauty

(C) = Charm

_____ 1. Catching your reflection in the mirror every chance you get and primping.

_____ 2. Making a habit of walking by your crush's locker every day.

_____ 3. Complimenting the guys who are playing sports during PE but never saying anything to the girls who are doing well.

_____ 4. Reading your Bible each day.

_____ 5. Trying something on in the dressing room and wondering first if the guys will think it looks good on you.

_____ 6. Praying and talking to God throughout the day.

_____ 7. Flirting with the guys your friends like.

_____ 8. Obsessing over your hair and clothes all the time.

_____ 9. Praising God throughout the day for the many blessings He's given you.

ANSWERS: 1, B; 2, C; 3, C; 4, A; 5, C; 6, A; 7, C; 8, B; 10, A.

Week 32:
Run for the Prize

Bible Reading

Therefore, since we also have such a large cloud of witnesses surrounding us, let us lay aside every weight and the sin that so easily ensnares us. Let us run with endurance the race that lies before us, keeping our eyes on Jesus, the source and perfecter of our faith.
—Hebrews 12:1-2

Read the passage aloud and listen carefully for the answers to the following questions:

What two things should we lay aside in the race?

_____

_____

What should we keep our eyes on when running the race?

_____

Bringing It Home

Michaela watched as her youth minister demonstrated how hard it was to run a race while wearing a backpack filled with bricks. He struggled as he attempted to lift the backpack up off the ground and place it on his back. He was hunkered down as he struggled step-by-step to the finish line he had drawn at the end of the parking lot. He only made it about ten feet before he let the backpack fall to the ground with a loud thud. He then invited the students to come up one at a time, to try to lift the backpack and see how heavy it was.

After that, he asked if there were any volunteers who thought they could make it to the finish line with the backpack on their backs—and one of the guys raised his hand. He struggled to even get the backpack on his back, and as he struggled toward the finish line, the youth minister told him that he was going to get some of the students on the sidelines

to randomly step in and try to trip him as he passed by. The boy knew he didn't stand a chance and gave up.

Michaela's youth minister explained that every time we cave in to sin, it is like adding a brick to the backpack. And when we hang out with people who lead us down the wrong path or try to trip us up, we can't stay focused on the finish line. He reminded them that Jesus stands at the finish line and is the prize we run for in this world. Michaela had never really thought about "running the Christian race" in that way before. Later that night, she prayed and asked God to show her the things that were slowing her down in the race; and she asked Him to help her lay those things aside so she could keep her eye on the *real* prize—Jesus!

What does God's Word say?

God reminds us that the real prize for the Christian at the end of the race is eternal life. When we keep our eyes on the finish line, we remember what we're running for—a heavenly prize, not an earthly prize. This race on earth is a marathon, not a sprint. Marathons are challenging, and at times, the course will be challenging too. Our sins may weigh us down, but when we focus on Jesus at the finish line, we remember what He did. He carried our sins to the cross and paid the penalty for them, so we don't have to carry them any longer.

Sometimes other people can weigh us down or knock us off the racecourse. This is why it's important to have friends who are focused on the same heavenly prize we are. God's Word reminds us that it will take "endurance" to run the race well. *Endurance* means "the ability or strength to continue or last." If we want to last in the race, we'll need to stay in shape and listen to our Trainer. He knows the racecourse better than anyone and can give us the endurance we need to finish the race well. To understand Him, we need to be in His Word. The Bible is our map for the race.

Think About It

Have you ever thought of the Christian journey as a race?

Talk About It

Questions to ask your mom:

When you were my age, what were some things that ensnared you or knocked you off course in the race?

If life is like a race, do you care more about running for worldly prizes or running for a heavenly prize (eternal life)? What are some ways you can keep your eyes on Jesus in the race?

_____

_____

_____

_____

Questions for your mom to ask you:

Right now, would you say you care more about running for worldly prizes or a heavenly prize? What are some ways you can keep your eyes on Jesus in the race?

_____

_____

_____

_____

What are some things that have ensnared you or knocked you off course in the race?

This Week

The best way to "lay aside every weight and the sin that so easily ensnares us" is to confess our sins on a regular basis. For example, when you are going to bed at night, take a few minutes during your prayer time to confess (admit) the sins you committed that day. Thank God for His forgiveness, and ask Him to help you stay strong. Try it each night this week, and when you do, picture Jesus taking that sin and placing it at the foot of the cross. If it's at the cross, you don't have to carry it!

Keep Going

Unscramble the words below to discover ways to build endurance for the Christian race.

___ ___ ___ ___   ___ ___ ___ ___   ___ ___ ___ ___ ___
A   R   E   D   R   U   Y   O   L   B   B   E   I

___ ___ ___ ___
R   Y   A   P

___ ___ ___ ___ ___ ___   ___ ___ ___ ___ ___
T   N   A   T   D   E   H   R   C   C   U   H

___ ___ ___ ___ ___ ___ ___ ___ ___ .
G   E   Y   R   R   L   U   A   L

____ ____ __

S I T L N E   O T

_____ _____

S I C R A H T N I   M S I C U

__ _____

O D   O L O S A N V D E T I

____ _____!

K E I L S T H I

243

Week 33:
The Greatest Gain

Bible Reading

But everything that was a gain to me, I have considered to be a loss because of Christ. More than that, I also consider everything to be a loss in view of the surpassing value of knowing Christ Jesus my Lord.

—Philippians 3:7-8

Read the passage aloud and listen carefully for the answers to the following questions:

What is a loss because of Christ?

_____

_____

What has greater value in our lives than anything the world has to offer?

_____

_____

Bringing It Home

Becca stood in her brother Josh's room and looked around. He had been away at college for over three years now, but when she missed him, it helped to go in his room and take in the reminders. She smiled as she thought about the times he would shoo her out and tell her, "Get outta here, punk." She always knew he was kidding. Her brother had always been the kind of big brother every little sister dreams of having. Sure, she still got to see him when he came home to visit, but it wasn't quite the same.

The night before, Josh and her dad had gotten in a huge fight over the phone, and Josh had texted her to explain why. He knew she would be concerned. He told her he was thinking about doing mission work outside of the country after college, but Dad had lost it when Josh brought it up. She had heard her dad shout during the call, "You graduated at the top of your high school class and won more academic awards than most kids can ever hope for, and you want to waste all that hard work?! I don't get it!"

As she looked at Josh's trophies, plaques, and ribbons lining his bookshelves, she could understand where her dad was coming from. Josh was the kind of kid who, according to teachers and friends and others who knew him, could change the world. She was pretty sure they thought he could use his knowledge to cure cancer or invent some type of life-changing technology. Instead, he was planning to apply his engineering skills toward figuring out a way to bring water purification systems to remote parts of the world—to the people who didn't have access to clean water and suffered from many diseases. He explained to her that he wanted to use the knowledge God had blessed him with in order to tell others about Jesus.

Maybe he was the kind of kid who could change the world—but he had something more important than just knowledge. If knowing Jesus really was the most important thing in the world, who was she to argue with Josh's decision?

What does God's Word say?

God's Word reminds us that nothing in this world is more valuable than knowing Christ. Absolutely nothing. Sometimes that truth is hard to remember because the focus in this world is to gather up as many worldly prizes, achievements, possessions, and awards as possible. We are easily impressed by big houses, famous people, and fancy things, but how much is that really worth if we don't know Christ? Paul (the apostle who spoke this truth in the Bible verse) knew that people would chase after worldly prizes, so he reminded us of the truth that anything other than knowing Christ is a loss. This doesn't mean that honors, possessions, and achievements are bad things. God gives us the ability to have these things. But the verse reminds us that knowing Christ should be our greatest priority and focus.

As you get older, you will come across many examples of people looking for worth and value in things other than Jesus Christ. Sadly, some of these people are Christians who possess the greatest treasure imaginable, but instead, they chase after other treasures while neglecting their relationship with Christ. We must always be on guard so that we do not begin to believe the lie that anything the world has to offer is more valuable than knowing Christ. And *knowing* Christ is much different from just *believing in* Christ. To know someone requires spending time with them. What about you? What are you chasing after?

Think About It

Do you consider everything in your life a loss compared to the value of knowing Christ?

Talk About It

Questions to ask your mom:

Is it hard for you to remember that everything is a loss compared to knowing Jesus as Lord? What helps you remember this truth?

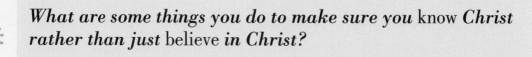

What are some things you do to make sure you know *Christ rather than just* believe *in Christ?*

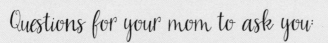

Questions for your mom to ask you:

What are some things that kids your age consider valuable? (Give a few examples.)

_____

_____

_____

_____

What are some things you are doing to "know Christ" better?

_____

_____

_____

_____

This Week

Think through your worldly gains (awards, honors, possessions, etc.). What are your top-five greatest gains? List them below. Now, write out Philippians 3:7–8. Do you consider your gains a loss compared to knowing Christ? If so, write the word *loss* beside each one.

Keep Going

Look at the list below and determine which ones are a "loss" and which ones are a "gain" according to Philippians 3:7–8. Circle your choice.

You made a 100 on the weekly spelling test.
Loss   *Gain*

You just got the lead in the upcoming school play!
Loss   *Gain*

You and your family belong to a wonderful church, and you learn so much in your class on Sunday mornings.
Loss   *Gain*

You finally saved enough money for a new tablet and can't wait to go pick it out!
Loss   *Gain*

Your family is going on a mission trip this summer and will be able to share Christ with many who don't know Him.
Loss   *Gain*

You and your mom are going through this devo each week!
Loss   *Gain*

For your birthday you got the fur-lined boots you had been begging your parents to get you!
Loss   *Gain*

You and one of your friends are reading through a book of the Bible together.
Loss   *Gain*

Week 34:
Made by God

Bible Reading

I will praise You because I have been remarkably and wonderfully made. Your works are wonderful, and I know this very well.

—Psalm 139:14

Read the passage aloud and listen carefully for the answers to the following questions:

Why should we praise God?

_____

_____

His works are what?

_____

_____

Bringing It Home

Maisie felt uncomfortable as Kylie's older sister snapped at Kylie when they stopped for frozen yogurt on the way home from the movie. "Seriously, Kylie, ease up or you'll be as big as a house by the time you're my age. Do you want to be fat?" Maisie and Kylie always got the crushed candy topping and lots of rainbow sprinkles when they came here, so what was the big deal? Maisie felt bad for Kylie, and Maisie could tell her friend was embarrassed because her face always turned red when she was. She tried to comfort Kylie and told her to ignore her sister. Maisie was taller and heavier than Kylie, so she knew Kylie's sister was probably talking to her too. Whatever. Kylie's sister could be so mean sometimes.

Maisie's mom and grandmother were curvier than most women, and she knew she would probably have a similar body shape when she got older. She was fine with it and loved the way they looked. She wished

Kylie could feel as good about herself as Maisie did. Maisie's mom had warned her that she might feel pressure to look a certain way as she got older, but the important thing to remember was to take care of herself and be healthy.

The crazy thing was, Maisie didn't even think Kylie's sister looked healthy! She was super skinny, and Kylie said she was on a diet all the time because she was so afraid of gaining weight. Maisie planned to talk to Kylie about her sister's comment later, to reassure her it was possible to be healthy and still have some rainbow sprinkles on the side!

What does God's Word say?

Think about how boring it would be if God made everyone the same exact size and shape. Instead, He made each one of us unique and different. Unfortunately, many of the female models you see in ads, on TV, and in movies have a small frame and tend to be very thin. The truth is, that body shape only represents a tiny percentage of girls and women. For that reason, many girls believe only one body size and shape is acceptable; and sadly, they are unable to appreciate the unique person God created them to be.

God wants us to take care of the bodies He gave us, but that doesn't mean we have to all look alike and weigh the same. Just as God created a variety of skin colors, eye colors, hair colors, and other features that vary from person to person, He also created people to be different sizes and shapes. He wants us to not only accept our differences, but appreciate them as well. In fact, we are told to "praise Him" for our being "remarkably and wonderfully made." Do you appreciate the way God made you? Do you believe you are a unique and beautiful creation? Girls who "know this very well" are not likely to believe the lie that they need to look a certain way. They are happy to be themselves and don't try to be someone they are not.

Think About It

Are you happy with the way
God made you?

Talk About It

Questions to ask your mom:

When you were my age, did you feel good about the way God made you?

If so, why is that? If not, what has helped you see yourself through God's eyes?

_____

_____

_____

_____

_____

Questions for your mom to ask you:

Are you able to say you are "remarkably and wonderfully made"? Why or why not?

_____

_____

_____

_____

Have you felt pressure to look a certain way? If yes, how so?

This Week

Be on the lookout for messages around you that suggest girls and women should be a certain body shape and/or weight. Maybe it's an ad you see on TV or a comment someone makes. Try to write them down in your journal and tally them up at the end of the week to see how many times you were exposed to the lie. (PS: Tell your mom to do the same thing, and compare your results at the end of the week!)

Keep Going

(Note: This would be a good activity to do with your mom!)

Do one or both of the following activities:

1. Find a women's magazine. Start at the very beginning and go through page by page. Tear out each page that has a picture of a woman, whether it's an ad or an article. (Make sure you have permission from your mom first!) When you reach the end, go back through the images and list all the similarities the pictures share when it comes to body shape and weight. Do you see one type represented? What message do you think this suggests to girls?

_____

_____

_____

2. Ask your mom to help you find a popular online clothing shop for tween or teen girls. Look through the images of models and list the similarities they share when it comes to body shape and weight. Do you see one type represented? What message do you think this suggests to girls?

_____

_____

Week 35:
Time for a Workout!

Bible Reading

Rather, train yourself in godliness, for the training of the body has a limited benefit, but godliness is beneficial in every way, since it holds promise for the present life and also for the life to come.
—1 Timothy 4:7-8

Read the passage aloud and listen carefully for the answers to the following questions:

What should we train ourselves in?

_____

_____

This training holds promise for two things. What are they?

_____

_____

_____

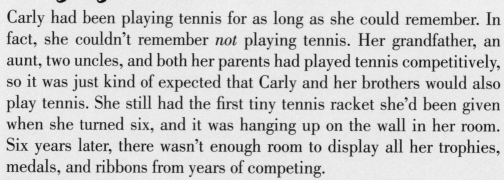

Bringing It Home

Carly had been playing tennis for as long as she could remember. In fact, she couldn't remember *not* playing tennis. Her grandfather, an aunt, two uncles, and both her parents had played tennis competitively, so it was just kind of expected that Carly and her brothers would also play tennis. She still had the first tiny tennis racket she'd been given when she turned six, and it was hanging up on the wall in her room. Six years later, there wasn't enough room to display all her trophies, medals, and ribbons from years of competing.

She loved the sport, but at the same time, she was weary of the training. Every day after school, they headed to the courts to meet with her coach. Her parents had even hired a private coach to help her with her serve. Sometimes, she heard them talking quietly about how much money they had spent on her training. They didn't seem to regret it because they kept signing her up. And she was good. Really good.

As she looked around her room at all the awards, she wondered how she could break the news to them that she needed a break from training. It was getting harder and harder to fit all her training in *and* keep her grades up. Not to mention, she was missing out on hanging out with her friends and being involved in her church youth group. As a sixth grader, she and her friends had just graduated from the children's department to the youth group, and she loved her youth minister. Her parents were involved in church, so she hoped they would understand if she needed to take a break from tennis.

What does God's Word say?

As you get older, you will notice that many people seem to be more concerned with the "training of the body" than the "training of the soul." God's Word tells us that both types of training have benefits, but the training of the body is not nearly as valuable as training in godliness. For example, if you eat right and exercise on a regular basis, your body will be healthier. You might even add years to your life if you continue to stay in shape. However, the benefits of exercise and nutrition end at the grave.

That is why God tells us to worry more about training ourselves in godliness. We experience the benefits of a godly life while we are here on this earth, but we will experience the greatest benefit of all when we reap the reward of eternal life (a life that continues beyond the grave). Of course, no one is perfect, and we will all make mistakes along the way; but those who train in godliness work hard to follow the teachings of the Bible and be more like Christ in everything they say and do. Look at it this way: Our Trainer is God, and our workout plan is to read the Bible (on a regular basis) and pray (stay in touch with our Trainer). How is your workout going?

Think About It

Do you think tween and teen girls are more concerned with their bodies being in shape or their souls being in shape?

Talk About It

Questions to ask your mom:

When you were my age, did you train yourself in godliness? If so, how?

_____

_____

_____

_____

_____

What are some examples of ways women place more focus on training of the body than on training in godliness? What is more important to you?

_____

_____

_____

_____

_____

Questions for your mom to ask you:

When it comes to the pop stars and celebrities the girls your age look up to, are they more focused on the training of the body or training in godliness? Share an example.

_____

_____

_____

_____

_____

What are you doing to train in godliness?

_____

_____

_____

_____

_____

_____

_____

This Week

Pay attention this week to messages you hear that encourage training our bodies or training in godliness. Maybe it's an ad on TV. Maybe it's something your pastor says on Sunday morning. Whatever it is, write it down. At the end of the week, tally up the number of times you heard messages about training the body and the number of times you heard about training in godliness. Which type of message did you hear more?

Keep Going

Look at the list below of ways to train in godliness, and come up with a workout plan to help you get in better shape (spiritually!). If you are already doing some of these things, fill them in on your weekly workout sheet on the next page. (Note: You don't need to fill in all the blanks!) If there are things you would like to do that you aren't currently doing, talk to your mom or dad about adding them to your schedule.

Read your Bible

Pray

Attend church

Attend Sunday school/youth group

Listen to Christian music

Memorize a Bible verse

Attend a weekly Bible study

Read a Christian book

Start a family devotional and prayer time

Volunteer or do mission work

Go through a devotional (this one counts!)

Read a psalm

Read a proverb

Sunday

Monday

Tuesday

Wednesday

Thursday

Friday

Saturday

Week 36:
One Way

Bible Reading

Jesus told him, "I am the way, the truth, and the life. No one comes to the Father except through Me."

— John 14:6

267

Read the passage aloud and listen carefully for the answers to the following questions:

Jesus said He is the way, the truth, and the what?

He also said that no one comes to the Father (God) except how?

Bringing It Home

"Everyone goes to heaven. I mean, as long as you're a good person and you don't commit murder, I'm pretty sure you get in." Jenna remained silent while Mallory shared with the girls at the sleepover about her personal view on heaven. One of the other girls had brought the topic up, and Mallory didn't hesitate to chime in and assure everyone there was no need to worry. Jenna hated that the other girls might believe Mallory, but she wasn't sure what to say. Some of her friends at the sleepover practiced different religions, and a couple of them said they didn't even believe in God. She didn't want to hurt anyone's feelings, but she also knew that by remaining silent about the truth, some girls would be misled about heaven and eternal life (life after death).

Jenna's Sunday school teacher had told her class that it was important to know how to talk about your beliefs with others in a way that wouldn't be rude or hurtful, but up until now, she hadn't really been in a situation where her beliefs were being challenged. Jenna had never questioned her beliefs before, but she knew many of her friends had not

grown up going to church and learned about Jesus. She couldn't imagine why anyone would not love Jesus if they knew what He had done for them—but that was the problem. How would they know if someone didn't tell them?

She said a silent prayer and asked God to help her represent the truth about Christ in a way that was kind and respectful. "Well, the truth is, there is only one way to get into heaven." The girls grew silent, and all eyes were on Jenna. She took a deep breath and continued. "This isn't easy for me to say because I know some of you don't believe in Jesus. I don't want to pick a fight. I want to tell you the truth because I care about you. The truth is . . . the only way to God and heaven is by believing in His Son, Jesus." Jenna felt a peace and calm come over her that she knew was from God as she continued to share.

What does God's Word say?

One of the biggest lies you will hear as you get older is that there are many paths to reach God. You may also hear the lie that all faiths worship or believe in the same God. This is also not true. Jesus Himself said, "I am the way, the truth, and the life. No one comes to the Father except through Me." If there were other ways to reach God, Jesus would have said so—but He made it clear that there was only one way: through Him. God cannot be reached through any other means. That is what it means to believe in the Christian faith. You can't "kind of" believe in Jesus. You either believe Him and take Him at His word, or you don't.

It may not seem kind to hold the belief that there is only one way to God (through a personal relationship with Christ), but we didn't make up the rules. God, our Creator, did. Those who believe there are other ways to reach God (and heaven) would have to conclude (believe) Jesus was lying when He claimed to be the only way. Many of those who believe

there are many paths to the same God often claim Jesus was a good, moral teacher. The problem is, He can't be a good and moral teacher if what He claimed in John 14:6 is a lie. In other words, we must all decide if Jesus is a liar or Lord. He can't be both. Who do you say Jesus is?

Think About It

Before reading John 14:6, did you believe there were many paths to God (and heaven)?

Talk About It

Questions to ask your mom:

Have you had conversations with people who believe there are many ways to God? Share an example.

_____

_____

_____

_____

_____

How do you talk about Jesus to people who don't know Him?

_____

_____

_____

_____

_____

Questions for your mom to ask you:

Do you have friends who believe there are many ways to God? If yes, how did the subject come up?

_____

_____

_____

_____

_____

_____

_____

How do you talk about Jesus to people who don't know Him?

_____

_____

_____

_____

_____

_____

This Week

Take some time to read John 14:1–9 to better understand what Jesus said before and after verse 6. Pay careful attention to the verses where He mentions God (the Father).

What are some of the claims Jesus makes about Himself and the Father? (This is hard, so ask your mom to help you!)

Keep Going

True or False? Circle your choice. (Look back over John 14:1–9 for the right answer.)

1. As long as a person is a good person and tries to live a good life, they will go to heaven and spend eternity (life after death) with God.

   True   *False*

2. Jesus said, "No one comes to the Father except through Me, Buddha (the Hindu prophet), or Muhammad (the proclaimed Muslim messenger)."

   True   *False*

3. Thomas asked Jesus the question, "How can we know the way (to God)?" (John 14:5). Jesus answered, "Believe in whatever you want, and you will find Him."

   True   *False*

4. Jesus said, "If you know Me, you will also know My Father." His earthly parents were Mary and Joseph, so He was probably talking about Joseph.

   True   *False*

5. When Jesus said, "Believe Me that I am in the Father and the Father is in Me," He was lying. (John 14:11).

   True   *False*

ANSWERS: They are all false!

274

Week 37:
Heart of the Matter

Bible Reading

Trust in the LORD with all your heart, and do not rely on your own understanding; think about Him in all your ways, and He will guide you on the right paths.
—Proverbs 3:5-6

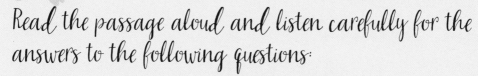

Read the passage aloud and listen carefully for the answers to the following questions:

We should trust in the Lord with what?

_____

If we think about Him in all our ways, He will guide us on what?

_____

Bringing It Home

Charlotte had no idea what to do. She got a blank piece of paper and marker out of her desk and drew a line down the center of the page from top to bottom. At the top of one column, she wrote, "Reasons to Stay," and at the top of the other column, she wrote, "Reasons to Leave." All year she had begged her parents to allow her to go to the public school all her neighbor friends attended. She had been at the same private school since kindergarten, but she felt like she was ready for a change.

Her parents had resisted the idea at first, but after a few months of thinking about it, they decided to look into it. They had visited the school and were really impressed with the teachers and the academic performance record. Charlotte had even shadowed for a half day by attending a class in her grade. One of her best friends was in the class, so that made it even more fun. After getting a feel for the school, she told her parents she for sure wanted to go there next year. Her parents

prayed about it and told her they were comfortable with either school, and the decision was up to her.

She had a week to decide because they would have to register by a certain date. The week was up, and her parents needed to know her final decision by the next day. But as she thought more about leaving her old school and many of the friends she had known since kindergarten, she began to waver in her decision. As she looked at the columns she had drawn on the paper, she began to list the reasons to stay and the reasons to leave. She knew it was a huge decision, and she wished there was an easier way to decide!

What does God's Word say?

God wants us to trust Him with the details of our lives. He wants us to come to Him when we have doubts or fears. He wants to be the first person we turn to when we need direction in life. When facing a difficult choice, most people will make a decision based on what feels right at the time. The problem is, what feels right isn't always the right thing to do. For that reason, we shouldn't "rely on our own understanding."

If we make God our first thought, it will become second nature to turn to Him throughout our day. There is nothing we can't bring to God. He knows and understands our needs before we bring them up. It delights His heart when His children trust Him with the difficult choices of life, as well as the little details. Even if the path He guides us to is not a path we would have chosen, we can trust Him with the outcome because we have learned to turn to Him before anyone else.

Think About It

Do you look to God when facing a
difficult choice, or do you try to figure things
out on your own?

Talk About It

Questions to ask your mom:

**Can you think of a difficult choice you have faced recently?
What was it?**

Did you look to God for guidance? If yes, share some ways you sought God's wisdom.

Questions for your mom to ask you:

Can you think of a difficult choice you have faced recently? What was it?

Did you look to God for guidance? If yes, share some ways you sought God's wisdom.

_____

_____

_____

_____

_____

This Week

Make a list of the three most difficult choices you have faced in your life. (Have mom do this exercise too!) As you think back, did you look to God for answers?

Keep Going

Circle the things below that can help you trust in the Lord when facing difficult choices.

Talk to your best friend and get a second opinion.

Look up Bible verses about trusting God.

Pray and ask God to show you the right path to take.

Talk to God throughout the day when you find yourself doubting or worrying.

Ask God to give you peace about the situation.

Trust your gut.

Talk to someone who loves God and will give you godly advice.

Do what feels right at the time.

Google it.

Attend a Bible-believing church on a regular basis.

Ask other Christians to pray for your situation.

Find a Bible reading plan and try to read the Bible every day.

Go out for Chinese food and put your faith in the fortune cookie.

Week 38:
A New, Improved You

Bible Reading

Don't copy the behavior and customs of this world, but let God transform you into a new person by changing the way you think. Then you will learn to know God's will for you, which is good and pleasing and perfect.

—Romans 12:2 NLT

Read the passage aloud and listen carefully for the answers to the following questions:

We are not to copy the behavior and customs of what?

How are we transformed into a new person?

God's will for us is good and pleasing and what?

Bringing It Home

Tate and Malia had been best friends since preschool, but now it seemed they were drifting apart. Malia was no longer interested in doing the things they had always enjoyed before, and she was caught up in doing the things the popular kids liked to do. At first, it was the music. When they hung out, Malia insisted on listening to the top hits, but many of them had lyrics that had bad language and talked about inappropriate things. When Tate said something about it to her, Malia brushed it off and said, "Don't be such a baby! Everyone in our grade listens to this music." Tate didn't want to lose Malia as a friend, so she let it go.

But then Malia became obsessed with talking about the boys in their class. All. The. Time. Tate liked boys, but she had other things in her life that were more important. After that, it was the movies they watched. The last time Tate was at Malia's house, Malia wanted to watch an R-rated movie after her parents went to bed, but she got mad when Tate said Malia would have to watch it alone. On top of that, Malia was starting to wear makeup and talked about name-brand clothes all the time. Tate missed her friend and just wanted the old Malia back.

What does God's Word say?

As you are growing up, you will notice that most kids your age will want to follow the crowd more than they want to follow God. Very few will stop to even give much thought to God's good, pleasing, and perfect will. They will simply go with the flow. If their friends are wearing name brands, they will want to wear name brands. If their friends watch certain shows, they will want to watch them too—even if the content might be inappropriate. If their friends gossip about one another, chances are, they will also gossip about others.

Tweens and teens naturally want to follow the crowd and fit in. Unfortunately, it isn't always cool to follow God. Some of your friends may give you a hard time. When we choose to become believers (Christians), it also means we are committed to following God's ways rather than the ways of the world. The more we get to know God (read the Bible, pray, get involved in church activities, etc.), the more we will begin to think like Him. This is what it means when the verse says God will "transform you into a new person by changing the way you think."

Think About It

Do you think it's hard for tween girls to keep from copying the behaviors and customs of this world?

Talk About It

Questions for you to ask your mom:

When you were a tween/teen girl, was it a struggle for you not to copy the behaviors and customs of this world? Share a time when you gave in and followed the world's ways rather than God's ways.

Can you think of a time when God transformed you into a new person by changing the way you think? Share the example.

_____

_____

_____

_____

_____

Questions for your mom to ask you:

What are some ways girls your age try to copy the behaviors and customs of this world? Be specific.

_____

_____

_____

_____

Are you more of a crowd follower or a Jesus follower?

This Week

Be on the lookout this week for moments when you or your friends are tempted to copy the behaviors and customs of this world. (For example: if you put yourself before others, gossip, listen to inappropriate music, etc.) At the end of the week, look over the list and think of ways to be transformed, and try to change the way you think.

Keep Going

Take the quiz below to see if you are a crowd follower or a Jesus follower. Circle your answers.

1. You are hanging out with your friends, and one of them begins to say tacky things about a girl in your class. The other girls also chime in and say rude things. You . . .

   a. laugh, nod your head, and say, "Oh, my gosh, I know! She's so weird!"

   b. remain completely silent.

   c. say, "Guys, we wouldn't want other people to say these things about us. I think we should be nicer."

2. You are out of town at a weekend dance competition, and all the girls and moms are planning to go to a fun place for breakfast on Sunday morning before the final competition. You and your mom and dad usually find a place to go to church since you don't like to miss worship when you travel. You . . .

   a. get in a huge fight with your parents and tell them you're sick of missing out on all the fun stuff for church.

   b. complain to your friends about it, but go along with your parents and don't say anything.

   c. hate to miss the fun, but nothing is more important than worshipping God. You don't want anything to come before your relationship with Him, so you are excited to go to church and be reminded of what's most important in your life.

3. You and all of your friends are on social media now, but lately there has been so much drama. One of your friends posted a status and told her followers to tag someone they thought was annoying. Your name didn't get tagged, but some of your friends did. Now, of course, they are upset. You . . .

   a. figure it's part of being a tween, so you tag a few girls who you think are annoying. Maybe they'll get the hint.

   b. ignore it and don't take part in the latest drama.

   c. talk to your friend in private who posted the status, and encourage her to take it down. You remind her to think more about the feelings of others. If the drama continues, you might need to take a break from social media. You don't want anything to distract you from your relationship with the Lord.

How Did You Do?

If you chose mostly a's, you are a crowd follower! Pray and ask God to give you the courage to follow Christ rather than the crowd. You can do it!

If you chose mostly b's, be careful because you are caught in the middle when it comes to pleasing God and pleasing the world. Stand strong!

If you chose mostly c's, good job! You are more concerned with following Christ than following the crowd. Keep up the good work!

Week 39:
Are You a Peacemaker?

Bible Reading

Do not repay anyone evil for evil. Try to do what is honorable in everyone's eyes. If possible, on your part, live at peace with everyone.
—Romans 12:17-18

Read the passage aloud and listen carefully for the answers to the following questions:

Do not repay what for what?

If possible, we are called to do what?

Bringing It Home

Adrienne strongly disliked her PE teacher. She wasn't allowed to say she "hated" anyone, but if she *did* hate someone, it was Mrs. Robinson. Adrienne was pretty sure Mrs. Robinson felt the same way about her, because every day she got on to Adrienne for something. "Adrienne, are you talking again? Run around the backstop two times!" "Adrienne, you call that a jumping jack? Do twenty more!" "Adrienne, grab a basket and pick up all the tennis balls on the court. Go! You heard me!"

Grrrrr! Adrienne used to love PE, but not anymore. Mrs. Robinson had ruined it for her. The worst part was, she was only halfway through the school year and had Mrs. Robinson *again* for the second half!

Sometimes she would daydream about pranks she wanted to play on Mrs. Robinson. One of her friends told her about a fun prank she and her dad had played on her mom. When they went camping, her dad brought along a real-looking rubber snake and put it in the picnic basket. Later that day when her mom opened the lid, she screamed loud enough to be heard throughout the entire campground. *Hmm*, Adrienne thought. *I wonder if my friend still has that rubber snake?* Okay, she wouldn't really play that prank on Mrs. Robinson, but it was fun to think about it.

When she told her mom about how mean Mrs. Robinson was, her mom suggested that she try to make peace with her rather than get back at her. Ugh. It was so much easier to be mad. She wanted to treat Mrs. Robinson the same way Mrs. Robinson had treated her. But Adrienne's mom told her to pray about it every night that week, and to ask God to show her how to respond to Mrs. Robinson. She was pretty sure God wouldn't agree with her playing pranks—but then again, He didn't have Mrs. Robinson as a teacher!

What does God's Word say?

It is hard to be a follower of Christ. Believers are called to behave in a way that is pleasing to God, even in situations when they are treated unfairly. It's much easier to get revenge or blow up rather than keep our cool and react calmly with kindness and respect. The best example for how we are to behave in those situations is Jesus. When Jesus was sentenced to death, He was mistreated by many people. They cried for His death, shouting, "Crucify Him!" Keep in mind, Jesus had done nothing wrong! (He was without sin.)

But that wasn't all. The Roman soldiers mocked Him by putting a robe on Him and a crown of thorns on His head. They shouted, "Hail, King of the Jews!" as they spit on Him and beat Him with a reed. As if that wasn't enough, the chief priests, scribes, and elders, as well as a thief on the cross, mocked Him as He hung there dying. They taunted Him, saying, "If You are the Son of God, come down from the cross!" All the while, Jesus remained silent and did nothing.

Keep in mind, Jesus is the Son of God and had the power to zap them all dead—to repay evil for evil. At any time, He could have changed His mind and said, "Forget this. I'm not dying for these ungrateful people!" Yet instead, He chose to die for the sins of all mankind, including those who treated Him unfairly, those who insulted Him, and even those who sentenced Him to die.

Fortunately, God is not calling us to die for our enemies. He simply wants us to live at peace with everyone, including those who treat us unfairly or annoy us on a regular basis. Is that too much to ask . . . after all Jesus did?

Think About It

When someone treats you unfairly, is it hard for you to react in a way that promotes peace?

Talk About It

Questions to ask your mom:

When you were my age, did you ever have a situation when someone treated you unfairly and you wanted to get back at them? Did you take revenge?

_____

_____

_____

_____

Is it still hard at your age to live at peace with everyone? Share a recent example of a time where it was difficult.

_____

_____

_____

_____

Questions for your mom to ask you:

Have you ever had a situation when someone treated you unfairly and you wanted to get back at them? Did you take revenge?

_____

_____

_____

_____

What do you think the secret is to living at peace with everyone?

_____

_____

_____

_____

This Week

Take some time this week to think of someone who has a habit of treating you unfairly (or being annoying). Maybe it's a friend who teases you often, and you usually end up blowing up at her. Or maybe it's a brother or sister who is always taking your stuff without asking. Now, jot down a plan for how to react to them next time. How could you "live at peace" with the people on your list? (Note: Being a peacemaker doesn't necessarily mean you do or say nothing in a situation. The key is to react in a way that is peaceful rather than vengeful.)

Keep Going

Read the following situations and come up with a way to respond to each one in a way that would be "honorable in everyone's eyes."

1. You find out one of your friends shared a secret you told her in confidence. The same day you told her the secret, she shared with you the boy she has a crush on. **What is an honorable response?**

_____

_____

_____

_____

2. Your younger sister is always "borrowing" your things without asking for permission. Your mom told her that if she does it again, she'll be grounded for the day. Later, you find your tablet in her room. You know she has a sleepover to go to that night that she has really been looking forward to. **What is an honorable response?**

3. You have a volleyball game against the toughest team in the league. The girls are known for being bad sports, and during the game, you see why. While they are on the court, they taunt and tease you and your teammates, but not loud enough for the officials to hear them. To make it worse, they end up winning the game by one point. **What is an honorable response?**

Week 40:
Don't Miss Out

Bible Reading

The LORD is my shepherd; there is nothing I lack. He lets me lie down in green pastures; He leads me beside quiet waters. He renews my life; He leads me along the right paths for His name's sake.

—Psalm 23:1-3

Read the passage aloud and listen carefully for the answers to the following questions:

The Lord is our what?

_____

He leads us along what kind of paths?

_____

Bringing It Home

Rachel hadn't spent much time with God lately. She wasn't purposely avoiding God, but her mind had been preoccupied with other things—like her new tablet. She was one of the last girls in her friend group to get one, so she had a lot of catching up to do. And then there was dance team practice. She used to have class only once a week, but now that she had made the competitive team, she had practice three times a week and competitions on the weekends. Ugh—and then there was homework. It seemed like the older she got, the more distractions she had.

Spending time with God used to be easier. She used to pray regularly and talk to God throughout her day about everything from the latest girl drama going on at school to the upcoming dance competitions. Now that she was juggling so many different activities, she had gotten out of the habit of opening her Bible and praying. She felt guilty when she got on her tablet to chat with her friends or watch some silly YouTube video when she knew she hadn't made time for God. Technically, she had time for God, but she was distracted by other things that were competing for her attention.

She knew that her relationship with God was supposed to be the most important thing in her life, but lately, her actions weren't showing it. Her life had become so crowded and busy with other things. She knew she needed to make some changes, or more importantly, make room for God in her day—but she didn't know where to start. That night she prayed and told God how much she had missed spending time with Him. She asked Him to help her make her relationship with Him a priority in her life. She figured that was a pretty good start. The next day she woke up and resisted the urge to check her tablet to see if any of her friends had sent a message. What could be more important than opening up God's Word before a busy day at school?

What does God's Word say?

In the animal kingdom, sheep could not manage on their own without a shepherd to guide them. Shepherds guide sheep to green grass to make sure they get the proper nourishment they need. They lead their sheep to quiet or still waters to make sure they have enough to drink. If the waters are moving too quickly, the sheep could fall in and be weighted down by their woolly coats. Shepherds also guide their flocks to a resting place to keep them from getting too weary. A shepherd keeps a close eye on his flock and is ready to protect them from anything that might harm them. The sheep trust the shepherd because they know the shepherd will watch over them and guide them exactly where they need to go.

In the same way, the Lord is our Shepherd who lovingly takes care of us. When we get too busy or stray from His care, we are in danger. The nourishment He provides us is His Word, so we need to make sure we make time through the day to feed our souls. Our Shepherd also wants us to rest so that we don't grow weary with the burdens of life. If our days are filled with too many distractions and too much activity, we will

neglect our relationship with the Lord. When we aren't spending time with the Lord (our Shepherd), we may not know which paths to take. Just as the shepherd avoids the fast-moving streams and currents, the Lord wants to protect us from getting swept away in a fast-moving culture that could put us in danger. The world we live in is filled with many dangers, so it's important to stay in close contact with our Shepherd and trust Him to guide us along the right paths.

Think About It

Do you look to the Lord (your Shepherd) to lead you through your day?

Talk About It

Questions to ask your mom:

In what ways has the Lord been like a Shepherd in your life?

_____

_____

_____

_____

_____

What are some ways He helps you renew your life?

_____

_____

_____

_____

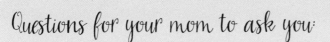

Questions for your mom to ask you:

What are some ways the Shepherd might lead His sheep beside quiet waters and away from the fast-moving current of today's culture?

Are you making time for the Shepherd each day? If not, what are some ways you can return to His care?

This Week

Write down Psalm 23:1–3. Each day, spend a few minutes trying to memorize the verses. As you get older and life gets busier, it will be a nice reminder to have tucked away in your heart.

Keep Going

Read Psalm 23 below. Then on the opposite page, circle the ways the Shepherd cares for us.

The LORD is my shepherd;
there is nothing I lack.
He lets me lie down in green pastures;
He leads me beside quiet waters.
He renews my life;
He leads me along the right paths
for His name's sake.
Even when I go through the darkest valley,
I fear no danger,
for You are with me;
Your rod and Your staff—they comfort me.
You prepare a table before me
in the presence of my enemies;
You anoint my head with oil;
my cup overflows.
Only goodness and faithful love will pursue me
all the days of my life,
and I will dwell in the house of the LORD
as long as I live.

The Shepherd

Leaves us alone in the pasture

Leads us along the right paths

Forgets to feed us

Never lets us lie down and rest

Prepares a table before us

Doesn't care about our needs

Leads us beside quiet waters

Makes us work all the time

Doesn't care when we're afraid

Walks with us through the darkest valley

Renews our life

Lets us get lost

Makes sure we lack nothing

Leads us to fast-moving streams to get a drink

Lets us lie down in green pastures

Renews our life

Week 41:
Rooted in God's Love

Bible Reading

I pray that from his glorious, unlimited resources he will empower you with inner strength through his Spirit. Then Christ will make his home in your hearts as you trust in him. Your roots will grow down into God's love and keep you strong.

—Ephesians 3:16–17 NLT

Read the passage aloud and listen carefully for the answers to the following questions:

Christ wants to make His home where?

What needs to grow down into God's love to keep us strong?

Bringing It Home

Jennifer couldn't remember a more frightening storm in all her ten years of living. The wind whistled and howled for hours. Her family huddled together in a bathroom of her home as the thunder roared and the rain poured down. The next morning when the storm had ended and all was quiet, she and her parents went outside to survey the damage. Their hearts sank when they saw the once tall, sturdy oak tree toppled over in the backyard. The tree had been there since they moved into the house when she was a baby, and it had provided a canopy of shade over their porch for all those years since. "Dad, how come our other trees survived the storm, but this one didn't?" Jennifer asked. Her dad slowly walked around the base of the tree, surveying the damage. As the tree lay on it side, you could see the roots of the tree that were exposed above the ground.

"A tree's survival depends on the roots. If the roots don't get enough water, they will weaken. When storms come and the wind blows hard, the tree won't be able to stand if the roots are weak," her father explained.

"But, the tree didn't look sick," she told her father. He went on to explain that trees need rain, and the drought they'd had for the past several years had robbed the tree of its nutrients, even though it looked perfectly fine above the soil. "You know, Jennifer, the Bible talks about how our roots should be nourished by God's love to keep us strong. When our roots are strong, we can survive any storm of life that may come our way." Jennifer thought hard about what her father was saying, and she wondered if her roots were strong enough to withstand the storms of life. It wasn't a matter of if the storms would come, but when. And she wanted to be prepared.

What does God's Word say?

You might not think it is a big deal to go to church, read your Bible, pray, and practice other spiritual disciplines, but it matters greatly when the storms of life come. Storms could be anything from divorced parents to a bully at school, a family member who is sick, or anything for that matter that causes you sadness, fear, or frustration. If you have taken care of your spiritual foundation by doing things that offer reminders of God's love, your roots will be stronger when the storms come. Rather than wait until the storm hits, it is best to build a storm shelter for the rainy days ahead.

We build a storm shelter by exposing ourselves to reminders of God's presence, His love for us, and His goodwill toward us. The more time we spend with God, the more prepared we are for the storms ahead. In fact, it is when the winds kick up and the rains pour that our faith is truly tested. Is it hard for you to trust God amid the storms of life? If so, you may not have a healthy root system. Take care of the roots because you will need to stay connected to the One who gives life and strength.

Think About It

Are you taking care of the roots
when it comes to your faith?

Talk About It

Questions to ask your mom:

Is your faith in God strong enough to withstand the storms of life? What do you do to strengthen your faith?

_____

_____

_____

_____

Have you experienced a storm that tested your faith? What was it?

_____

_____

_____

_____

Questions for your mom to ask you:

What are some ways your dad and I can help your roots grow deep in God's love?

_____

_____

_____

_____

_____

_____

Read Ephesians 3:18. Why do you think it's important to understand how wide, long, high, and deep God's love is for you?

_____

_____

_____

_____

_____

_____

This Week

With your mom's help and supervision, look up images on a computer or tablet of tree roots. Some of the images are drawings that show a mirror view of the tree canopy above the soil and the root system below the soil. Notice how the size of the root system is about the same size as the tree canopy. When it comes to being "rooted" in God's love, how might our spiritual foundation (what is in our heart) affect what others see on the outside?

Keep Going

Imagine that the tree below represents your heart. Label each of the roots with a way to go down deep into God's love. Draw more roots if you need to!

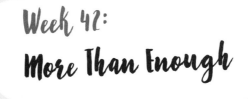

Week 42:
More Than Enough

Bible Reading

A thief comes only to steal and to kill and to destroy. I have come so that they may have life and have it in abundance.

— John 10:10

Read the passage aloud and listen carefully for the answers to the following questions:

Who comes "to steal and to kill and to destroy"?

_____

Jesus said He came so that we may have what?

_____

Bringing It Home

"I would be so happy if I lived in a house like this!" Lexie shrieked as she and her mom pulled up in front of her friend Scarlett's house. She knew it must be the right house because there was a huge birthday banner out front with Scarlett's name on it. One of her friends who had been to Scarlett's house before said that it had a gigantic home theater with real movie theater seats. It even had a concession stand with a popcorn maker and all kinds of snacks and drinks—and everything was free! She said the house even had an elevator. Scarlett never bragged about her house, but Lexie had guessed it must be pretty big when Scarlett told a story one day about how her little sister had gotten lost in the house when they first moved there. As Lexie walked up the brick stairway leading to the front door, she could certainly understand how someone could get lost in a house this size. It was huge!

When Lexie rang the doorbell, she was greeted by a woman in a uniform who welcomed her to the party and escorted her to the pool area out back. As Lexie followed the housekeeper, she couldn't help but stare

in amazement at each room they passed through. She almost felt guilty as she walked across the glossy, white floors for the dusty footprints she knew her flip-flops were probably leaving behind. It was almost like being in a museum where you could only look, but not touch. It was picture-perfect. And so very . . . white. Magazines were stacked neatly on glass tables, and candles burned in every room. Lexie laughed to herself as she thought about the damage her two-year-old little brother could do to a house like this. The glass tables and white sofas didn't stand a chance against his peanut-butter-smeared hands.

As she passed by the kitchen, she saw three more women dressed in uniforms who were arranging food on trays. Out back, the pool party was underway, and a live band with a DJ was playing their favorite songs. Scarlett's pool had a waterfall and a slide that was nicer than the one near Lexie's neighborhood pool. Lexie saw her friends lined up at the photo booth and ran over to meet them. She knew she would be remembering this party for a long time to come. Scarlett was so lucky. How could anyone be unhappy with a life like this?!

What does God's Word say?

If you look up the word *abundant* in the dictionary, you'll find it means "more than adequate" or "oversufficient." *Adequate* and *sufficient* mean just enough, so *abundant* means "more than enough." Who doesn't want a life that is "more than enough"? The problem is, our world believes an abundant life is a life with a bunch of money or material possessions. But Jesus wasn't talking about that kind of life. He was talking about something much better. The abundant life Jesus referred to is a life lived in pursuit of Him, rather than a life lived in pursuit of things. When we make our relationship with Christ more important than anything else this world has to offer, we will have a life that is more than adequate.

But the promises of an abundant life don't end there. A life lived in Christ will continue after we leave this world. Think about it. If you define the "abundant life" by money, riches, and things, you will be disappointed because even if you do have these things, you can't take any of them with you! First Timothy 6:7 says, "For we brought nothing into the world, and we can take nothing out." That doesn't mean it's a bad thing to have material blessings. However, it's wrong if we count on material blessings to bring us an abundant life. Only Christ can do that. If you want to have an abundant life, pursue Jesus before anything else.

Think About It

Do you want an abundant life?

Talk About It

Questions to ask your mom:

When you were my age, how did you define an "abundant life"?

_____

_____

_____

_____

How do you define it today?

_____

_____

_____

_____

Questions for your mom to ask you:

How do you think most kids your age would define an "abundant life"?

_____

_____

_____

_____

What are some things we can do to have the kind of abundant life Jesus was talking about?

_____

_____

_____

_____

_____

This Week

Read 1 Timothy 6:7–10 and John 10:10. What warning do the passages give those who want to be rich? Do you think that is one way the thief (the devil) comes "to steal and to kill and to destroy"? By leading people to believe money and things will give them an abundant life?

Keep Going

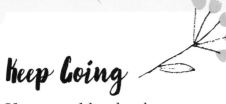

If you could only choose one option on each of the questions below, which would you rather have? Read each pair of options below, and circle your choice.

Would You Rather . . .

Belong to a country club or a church?

Own a big house on earth or have a mansion in heaven?

Have name-brand clothes or Jesus' name written on your heart (be a Christian)?

Spend all your birthday money on yourself or use some of it to give to your church or someone in need?

Take a tablet with only games or your Bible on a desert island for the day if you could only take one?

Talk to a friend or pray when you have a problem?

Be known as the girl who's popular or the girl who loves Jesus?

Go to on a summer vacation with a friend or a mission trip with a friend?

Have a hundred dollars or share your faith with someone who doesn't know about Jesus?

If you circled the first option more times than the second option, you are defining the "abundant life" all wrong and missing out on the abundant life Jesus was talking about in John 10:10. If you circled the second option more than the first, you are rich in Jesus!

Week 43:
God Is Good

Bible Reading

We know that all things work together for the good of those who love God: those who are called according to His purpose.

—Romans 8:28

All things work together for the good of those who what?

_____

And those who are called according to what?

_____

Bringing It Home

Molly had tears in her eyes as her mother shared the news that her grandfather was very sick and in the hospital. He was going to have an operation in a few days, and Molly was worried that the operation wouldn't help him get better. Her grandparents meant the world to her. They only lived a few miles from her home, and hardly a week went by that Molly didn't stop by their house. Her grandmother bought snacks for her and kept them in a special spot in the pantry where she could find them. She and her grandfather were especially close because he loved being outdoors just like Molly. They had even planted a garden in the backyard, and the tomatoes were starting to sprout on the vine. She didn't even like tomatoes, but she didn't tell her grandfather that. She was just happy to be spending time with him.

Her mother tried to assure her that many people had had the same operation her grandfather was going to have and that he was going to be all right. But Molly was still worried. She had never really thought about her grandparents not being a part of her life. She knew that the

Bible said that God works things together for His good, but she was struggling to see what the "good" was in her grandfather being so sick. She wanted to trust God with her fears, but it was really hard.

What does God's Word say?

Romans 8:28 is one of the most memorized verses in the Bible. As you get older, you will understand better why many people find encouragement in knowing that God works all things together for the good of those who love Him. Life can be hard. The verse doesn't mean that God will always work things out like we imagine. Everyone will experience difficult time and heartbreaks. However, God promises that He can take each and every painful event and bring *something* good from it. We may not see His goodness at the time we are experiencing the difficulty, but we can count on it.

For those who love God, we know that no matter what happens in this earthly life, we still have Him. He will never abandon us in our time of need. Our ultimate purpose (the main reason) we are here in this world is to glorify God and to point others to His love and forgiveness. That is our most important job. If we are called according to *that* purpose, rather than a purpose we imagined for ourselves, it will help us better understand when things don't play out in the way we thought they would.

Think About It

When things don't make sense, is it hard for you to trust God for the outcome?

Talk About It

Questions to ask your mom:

What are some of your Romans 8:28 moments in life?

_____

_____

_____

_____

Can you think of a time when you didn't understand why something was happening, but God later used it for His purpose? What was it?

_____

_____

_____

_____

Questions for your mom to ask you:

Do you have any Romans 8:28 moments? If so, share one.

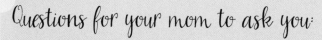

_____

_____

_____

_____

_____

_____

Is it hard for you to trust God even when your prayers aren't answered in the way you had hoped? What are some godly ways to respond?

_____

_____

_____

_____

_____

This Week

During this week, pay careful attention to situations you are going through that could use the encouragement of Romans 8:28. Or does someone you know need encouragement? Make a card and write down the verse to share it with that person. Also write it down for yourself, and hang the verse somewhere where it will be a reminder to you.

Keep Going

Read the situations below and imagine some "good" that could occur from a not-so-good situation.

1. Molly's grandfather is in the hospital and very sick. While he is there, the nurses on staff notice his strong trust and faith in God. One of the nurses has doubts about God.

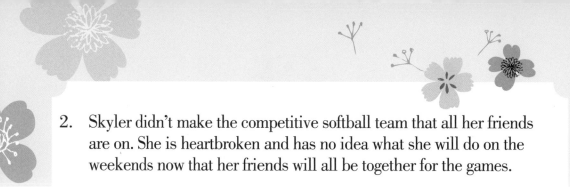

2. Skyler didn't make the competitive softball team that all her friends are on. She is heartbroken and has no idea what she will do on the weekends now that her friends will all be together for the games.

_____

_____

_____

3. Mary Catherine just found out her family is moving to another state. She cries herself to sleep that night and can't imagine how God can bring anything good out of this situation.

_____

_____

_____

4. Lyla's team has practiced so hard for the upcoming dance competition. They are sure they will win, but they end up not placing at all. The team that took first place walks by them as they are packing up to leave. They wave the trophy at them and rudely say, "Sorry, girls—better luck next time!"

_____

_____

_____

Week 44:
A Way of Escape

Bible Reading

God is faithful, and He will not allow you to be tempted beyond what you are able, but with the temptation He will also provide a way of escape so that you are able to bear it.
—1 Corinthians 10:13

Read the passage aloud and listen carefully for the answers to the following questions:

God is faithful and will not allow us to be tempted beyond what?

_____

With temptations, He will provide what?

_____

Bringing It Home

"C'mon, guys, let's take the shortcut!" Lily sighed when her friends started to follow after Camille down the wooded path that bordered their neighborhood. Her mother had finally given her permission to walk home with her friends after school, but there was one condition: She had to walk on the main sidewalk they had agreed on. There had been some vandalism in the park that ran along the edge of their neighborhood, and her parents felt it was safer to take the sidewalk path even though it was a longer route.

"Lily, are you coming?" Camille shouted as she continued down the path into the wooded park area. Lily didn't know what to do. She hated when she was the only one who wasn't allowed to do something her friends were allowed to do, and she knew Camille wouldn't understand. At that point, the girls figured something was up because Lily hadn't budged. "Guys, I can't," Lily finally stammered. "My parents won't let me go that way. They don't think it's safe." Whew, she said it. It felt good to be honest.

"Seriously, Lily? They will never know. Now hurry up!" Ugh. Camille didn't take no easily. Lily thought at least one of her friends would stand up for her and maybe walk home with her, but they all stood silently by Camille. "Sorry," said Lily. "I told you my parents' rule. I'm not going, so go without me. I'll see y'all tomorrow at school." She turned and began to walk down the sidewalk toward her house. She knew this was one of many temptations she would face as she got older, but she felt proud she had made the right choice on her own.

What does God's Word say?

God's Word tells us that the temptations we face are common to everyone. In other words, it's perfectly normal to have temptations in life. However, God assures us that the temptations we face will not be too much for us to handle. He will also give us a way out or a "way of escape." Sometimes it may seem easier to give in and follow the crowd, but the *easy way* is not always the *right way*. If we are to be followers of Christ, we must seek to behave in a way that is pleasing to Him. God gives believers the power and strength needed to make the right and good choice in a tempting situation.

Sometimes the way of escape may be to simply say no. Other times, you may need to walk away or call your mom or dad to come get you. Sometimes you may need to involve a teacher or a trusted adult. As you get older, it will be important to choose the kinds of friends who respect your decision to do the right thing. If you have a friend who often puts you in tempting situations or pressures you to do the wrong things, it's time to find a new friend.

Think About It

Do you think God cares about the temptations we face and gives us a way of escape?

Talk About It

Questions to ask your mom:

When you were my age, what kinds of temptations did you face?

Can you think of a temptation where God provided a way of escape and you took it?

_____

_____

_____

_____

_____

Questions for your mom to ask you:

What kinds of temptations have you faced this year?

_____

_____

_____

_____

Can you think of a temptation where God provided a way of escape and you took it?

_____

_____

_____

_____

_____

_____

This Week

Pay careful attention to tempting situations this week. Take note of temptations that students your age face, even if they don't involve you directly. You may not face too many temptations at this age, but as you get older, they will increase!

Keep Going

Take a look at the tempting situations below that are common to many tweens and teens, and see if you can figure out a "way of escape." If you're not sure what to do, ask your mom to help you.

Temptation: You are at a sleepover, and one of the girls pulls out her tablet and wants to show all the girls a website she found. By her description, you can tell it's very inappropriate. Most of the girls are circling around her to see the site. One of them asks if you are coming to see it.

Way of escape:

_____

_____

_____

_____

_____

Temptation: You are about to take the spelling test, and one of the girls sitting across from you tells you she forgot to study the night before. She asks you to push your tablet to the edge of your desk so she can see your answers.

Way of escape:

_____

_____

_____

_____

Temptation: One of your new friends asks you to go shopping with her. She wants to go into a store that has cute jewelry for a good price. She finds a cute necklace and whispers under her breath, "Do you know how easy it would be to take this? I do it all the time. Want me to get you something too?"

Way of escape:

_____

_____

_____

_____

Week 45:
Time to Pray

Bible Reading

Very early in the morning, while it was still dark, He got up, went out, and made His way to a deserted place. And He was praying there.
—Mark 1:35

Read the passage aloud and listen carefully for the answers to the following questions:

Where did Jesus go early in the morning, while it was still dark?

_____

What did He do there?

_____

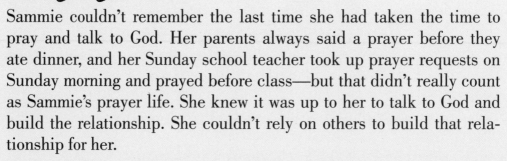

Bringing It Home

Sammie couldn't remember the last time she had taken the time to pray and talk to God. Her parents always said a prayer before they ate dinner, and her Sunday school teacher took up prayer requests on Sunday morning and prayed before class—but that didn't really count as Sammie's prayer life. She knew it was up to her to talk to God and build the relationship. She couldn't rely on others to build that relationship for her.

It wasn't that she didn't want to pray. It just seemed that when she tried, she would get distracted within seconds. Her phone would buzz. Or maybe the dog would bark to go outside. Or her favorite song would come on in the background, and she would lose track of what she'd been saying. Or if she prayed at bedtime, she would end up falling asleep. Her small-group leader had given them a challenge the week before to come up with a prayer plan and share it in class the next Sunday. He was also going to share some ideas to help them be more disciplined

when it came to a regular prayer time. Hopefully, she could find a plan that would work for her. Clearly, what she was doing wasn't working!

What does God's Word say?

Jesus knew the importance of talking to God, and He set the example for us by getting away from the crowds and finding a quiet place to give God His focused time and attention. As our lives become more complicated with technology and constant interruptions all around us, it has become a challenge for many people to be still and know God (Psalm 46:10). Yet, we need solitude (alone time), quiet, and stillness (away from distractions) to really hear from God. Prayer is about more than talking and giving God a wish list. It's a two-way relationship, so it also involves listening.

If you don't have a plan for prayer and you get easily distracted, try the ACTS plan. Each day (morning or night) find some time to get by yourself and talk to God by thinking of something to say in this order:

Adoration: Start by "adoring" God, which means praising Him for who He is. For example, thank God for being patient, loving, kind, and all-knowing.

Confession: The Bible instructs us to "confess" our sins, or to admit to the things we have done that are wrong. When you are praying, take a minute to confess the things you did wrong that day.

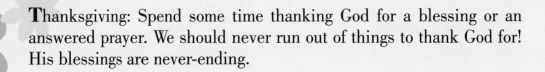

Thanksgiving: Spend some time thanking God for a blessing or an answered prayer. We should never run out of things to thank God for! His blessings are never-ending.

Supplication: A supplication is a request. Take a minute to pray for a situation or person. It could be anything from a sick family member to the big math test tomorrow at school.

You might have a different plan for prayer, but the important thing is to have a plan that works for you!

Think About It

How is your prayer life?

Talk About It

Questions to ask your mom:

Do you have a plan for prayer? If yes, what is it?

_____

_____

_____

_____

Is it hard for you to get away to a quiet place like Jesus did (find solitude) and hear from God? How can you make time with God a priority?

_____

_____

_____

_____

Questions for your mom to ask you:

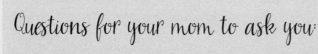

Are you easily distracted when you pray? If so, what are some of the distractions you experience?

_____

_____

_____

_____

_____

Do you have a plan for prayer? If yes, is it working? If not, do you think it's important to have one?

_____

_____

_____

_____

This Week

Find some time to pray and ask God to help you come up with a plan for prayer. Share the plan with your mom and ask her to check in with you from time to time to see how you're doing.

Keep Going

Find a quiet place free from all distractions where you can be completely alone. Write down your ACTS prayer below to get the hang of it. After that, try it every day for a week, and then keep on going!

Adoration:

_____

Confession:

_____

Thanksgiving:

_____

Supplication:

_____

Week 46:
This Little Light of Mine

Bible Reading

You are the light of the world. . . .
Let your light shine before men, so
that they may see your good works
and give glory to your Father
in heaven.
—Matthew 5:14, 16

Read the passage aloud and listen carefully for the answers to the following questions:

We are the light of what?

_____

Why should we let our lights shine?

_____

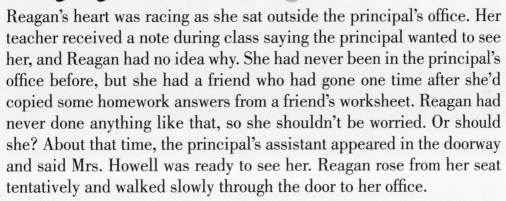

Bringing It Home

Reagan's heart was racing as she sat outside the principal's office. Her teacher received a note during class saying the principal wanted to see her, and Reagan had no idea why. She had never been in the principal's office before, but she had a friend who had gone one time after she'd copied some homework answers from a friend's worksheet. Reagan had never done anything like that, so she shouldn't be worried. Or should she? About that time, the principal's assistant appeared in the doorway and said Mrs. Howell was ready to see her. Reagan rose from her seat tentatively and walked slowly through the door to her office.

She breathed a sigh of relief when she saw the smile on Mrs. Howell's face. "Reagan, come in and have a seat. I'm sorry to pull you out of class, but I wanted to share some encouraging news with you." Reagan sat down in a chair in front of Mrs. Howell's desk and tried to contain her nervousness. "Reagan, I received a phone call this morning from the mother of a young lady who is in your homeroom class. She told me that it has been a challenge for her daughter to find new friends since moving here last month, but that you had gone out of your way to include her daughter and introduce her to your friends."

Reagan knew her cheeks were probably turning red as Mrs. Howell complimented her. "But that's not all, Reagan. I've also heard from several of your teachers about how kind you are to your fellow class-mates. I'm very proud of you." Reagan thanked Mrs. Howell for letting her know the good news. She could hardly contain the grin on her face as she left the principal's office. She had prayed at the beginning of the school year that she would be the kind of Christian who treats others like Jesus would treat them. She appreciated the compliment, but she felt like Jesus was the one who deserved the credit.

What does God's Word say?

Maybe you remember singing "This Little Light of Mine" when you were little. That song is based on this Bible passage. God wants us to live out our faith in the light for all to see. Others should look at us and know something about us is different. When the light of Christ lives in our hearts, we can't help but shine for Christ. Think of the many bene-fits of light. It helps us see in darkness.

Becoming a Christian should be the most wonderful thing that has ever happened to us. That is why God doesn't want us to keep the good news a secret. God tells us we are "the light of the world," but if we hide that light, how can others know Him? The goal is to behave as Jesus would and to point others to His goodness and grace.

"Hide it under a bushel? No! I'm gonna let it shine!" And PS—so should you!

Think About It

Would others be surprised to know you are a Christian? Or is it clear by the way you behave and treat others?

Talk About It

Questions to ask your mom:

In what ways do you "let your light shine before men"?

_____

_____

_____

_____

When others compliment your good works, how can you give the credit to God?

_____

_____

_____

_____

Questions for your mom to ask you:

What do you think Matthew 5:14 means when it says, "You are the light of the world"?

_____

_____

_____

_____

_____

Why do you think some Christians hide their light?

_____

_____

_____

_____

_____

This Week

Borrow your mom's or dad's smartphone and set the timer for five minutes. Find a really dark spot in your house. Maybe it's in a closet or your kitchen pantry, but make sure it's pitch-dark. If you need to, put a towel under the door to keep light from getting in. Leave the phone on the outside of the door, start the timer, and close the door. When you are sitting in the darkness, think about the benefits of light and how much we need it to survive in the world. Then take a minute to thank God for sending us Christ, the light of the world! Pray that you can bring that same light to those around you.

Keep Going

Look up the following verses to find the answers to the questions below. When you are done, see if you can find the key words in the seek-and-find puzzle.

John 8:12. Jesus said whoever follows Him will not walk in _____, but will have the light of _____.

Psalm 119:105. God's Word is a _____ to our feet and a light to our _____.

Isaiah 60:1. The light has come and the _____ of the Lord has risen upon us.

Acts 13:47. We have been appointed as a light to the Gentiles to bring _____ to the ends of the _____.

```
A  L  J  H  C  B  F  T  G  Q  O  O  A  M  W
P  J  U  U  X  C  A  G  K  I  W  G  G  E  E
I  E  Q  R  M  T  N  O  I  T  A  V  L  A  S
T  R  M  Z  E  I  A  O  J  N  K  Y  W  E  T
U  G  T  B  Q  A  C  X  X  I  C  C  R  H  T
I  T  M  C  Y  L  R  Y  C  T  Z  Q  C  M  A
B  J  E  R  U  D  K  T  O  F  S  B  Q  D  Y
Z  F  O  B  Q  M  U  Z  H  G  S  G  P  C  R
E  L  E  K  E  U  N  Q  U  P  E  Z  A  Z  J
G  D  L  I  F  E  J  X  J  L  N  O  T  M  K
O  R  L  E  E  F  P  E  K  L  K  G  H  B  Q
K  M  U  F  Z  M  L  Z  O  K  R  Y  Y  O  I
W  X  U  K  A  J  E  Y  B  P  A  D  F  U  I
Q  G  O  L  R  X  Z  D  R  E  D  D  C  E  S
N  C  Q  B  L  M  Z  F  X  I  J  V  K  Y  Z
```

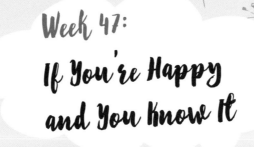

Week 47:
If You're Happy and You Know It

Bible Reading

In any and all circumstances I have learned the secret of being content—whether well fed or hungry, whether in abundance or in need. I am able to do all things through Him who strengthens me.

—Philippians 4:11-13

Read the passage aloud and listen carefully for the answers to the following questions:

The apostle Paul said he has learned to be content in what circumstances?

_____

He said he has learned the secret to contentment. What is it?

_____

Bringing It Home

When Autumn's parents told her they had signed up to go on the church mission trip over spring break, she was furious. Every year they went to the beach over spring break and stayed in a nice condo, but this year they were going to be staying in a nasty old hotel that didn't even have a pool! Not that it mattered. They were going to be working the whole time they were there. For weeks she whined and complained. "Why do we have to spend the entire break doing hard work when we could be at the beach?!" She had begged and pleaded with her parents to change their minds, but they were determined to go. They were going to help a very poor community several hours outside of her hometown, and her parents told her they thought it would be good for her to help others who were less fortunate. Whatever. What would be good for her was to be at the beach with her friends!

When the day of the trip arrived, Autumn pouted most of the way. Most of her friends were on their way to the beach, and all she could think about was how unfair her life was. When they arrived, they were given the assignment of building a playscape for the children in the community. They were told that the kids didn't have a park or place to gather and play. All week long, they worked alongside several other families to get it ready for the big opening day. As the week went on, Autumn began to feel a real pride in being able to take part in such a worthy project. She noticed many of the neighborhood kids gathering to watch their progress, and she could see the excitement on their faces.

Finally, the day arrived to open the park. A line of parents and kids waited at the entrance. Autumn would never forget the chorus of laughter and excitement as the children rushed through the gates to play on the playscape she had helped build. The children taught her an important lesson that week. Though they had little in the way of possessions, they were more content than many of the people Autumn knew that had much. When her family loaded up the car to leave the next day, Autumn hated to go. And to think she hadn't wanted to come!

What does God's Word say?

Sometimes we imagine that discontentment is experienced only in times of need or when we have little, but Paul reminds us that we can also be discontent in times of abundance or when we have a lot (Philippians 4:12). In fact, as you get older you will witness many examples of people who, in spite of being blessed abundantly, are miserable. It doesn't matter how much they have; they want more. It doesn't matter how well things are going in their lives; they will focus on the one thing that isn't going as well. We all have a tendency to be discontent, but Paul points out that our circumstances don't determine our happiness. We do.

Happiness or contentment is a choice. Just as Paul had to "learn" to be content, so do we. It requires an attitude adjustment. Instead of allowing his circumstances to make him bitter and unhappy, Paul chose to believe Christ would give him the strength needed to endure "any and all" circumstances. His happiness and contentment was tied to Christ rather than his situation. In other words, he refused to allow his circumstances to have the power to rob him of his happiness. He trusted Jesus more than an outcome. *That* was Paul's secret to finding happiness. And it can be yours too!

Think About It

What brings you contentment (happiness)?

Talk About It

Questions to ask your mom:

How do you struggle with contentment "in any and all circumstances"?

_____

_____

_____

Can you think of an example of when you struggled with being content in abundance? How about when you were in need?

_____

_____

_____

_____

Questions for your mom to ask you:

Do you think it's easier to have contentment "in abundance" or "in need"? Why?

Is it hard for you to be content "in any and all circumstances"? What could you do to become more content?

This Week

Whenever you are feeling discontent, stop and pray. Ask Christ to help you with an "attitude adjustment." After you pray, think of three things you are grateful for and thank God for them. You might even write them down in a journal and look back over them from time to time. Just as Paul learned contentment in "any and all" circumstances, you can too!

Keep Going

Read 2 Corinthians 11:24–27 to discover some of the "circumstances" Paul faced. Make a list of ten of them below. (Hint: There are twenty if you list each one separately!)

1. _____   6. _____

2. _____   7. _____

3. _____   8. _____

4. _____   9. _____

5. _____   10. _____

Read back over the list. Do you think you could find contentment if you had experienced Paul's same circumstances? Be honest!

Week 48:
No Greater Love

Bible Reading

For God loved the world in this way: He gave His One and Only Son, so that everyone who believes in Him will not perish but have eternal life.
— John 3:16

Read the passage aloud and listen carefully for the answers to the following questions:

In what way did God show His love to the world?

_____

_____

Those who believe in Jesus, the One and Only Son of God, will receive what?

_____

Bringing It Home

"Dad, why are those people holding up that sign with a Bible verse on it?" Sierra asked her father as they watched their favorite team play football. "I see that verse all the time during games. How come?" Sierra didn't really go to church, so she wasn't familiar with the Bible verse. She figured it must be important since it seemed to show up at so many different sporting events. Her dad explained that people hold it up because they want others to be curious about what it says, so they'll look it up in their Bibles. *Well, it certainly worked!* she thought. Sierra pulled out her phone and typed John 3:16 into the search engine. Up popped the verse:

"For God loved the world in this way: He gave His One and Only Son, so that everyone who believes in Him will not perish but have eternal life."

The older Sierra got, the more curious she was becoming about God. Most of her friends went to church and knew a lot more about God than she did. *I bet they would know what this verse means*, she thought. She knew God's Son was Jesus and that He had died on a cross, but she wasn't sure why that had to happen. *Why would God allow His Son to die?* she wondered. *And what exactly am I supposed to believe about Him?* She had so many questions.

If anyone would know the answers to her questions, it would be her cousin Jenna. Jenna had gone to church her whole life and knew a ton about God and the Bible. She quickly texted Jenna a picture of the sign and said, "Tell me what this means sometime." Jenna texted back within minutes and said, "That's my favorite Bible verse! I can't wait to talk to you about it!" Sierra figured there was a reason she saw the verse on the sign at the game. Who knows—maybe it was God!

What does God's Word say?

John 3:16 is one of the most popular Bible verses among Christians. It sums up the gospel of Christianity: God loves us and wants a relationship with us. Our sin stands in the way of God having a relationship with us because He is holy and pure and, therefore, cannot be in the presence of sin. The Bible says there must be a "blood sacrifice" to take away the stain of sin. In the Old Testament times (before Jesus was born into the world), the people would offer animals as a sacrifice in order to "pay for the sins of the people." They did this on a regular basis because they continued to sin. That was why they always were in need of a sacrifice.

John 3:16 is a reminder that God loves us even though we are sinners. But that's not all. He also desires to have a relationship with us. He didn't want us to have to keep presenting animal sacrifices, so He came up with a permanent sacrifice to cover our sins once and for all. He sent Jesus, His One and Only Son, to be the sacrifice for our sins; and all He asked in return was that we believe in His Son. When we say we are a "Christian," we are saying we believe that John 3:16 is true and Jesus is the only One who can pay for our sins and make it possible for us to have a personal relationship with God. In addition, we are guaranteed eternal life. That means that when we die, we will go to heaven and live forever with God. No wonder we see this verse on so many signs. People want to share the good news!

Think About It

Have you ever seen John 3:16 on a sign at a game or event before?

Talk About It

Questions to ask your mom:

What does John 3:16 mean to you? Do you believe it's true?

_____

_____

_____

_____

When did you believe in or put your trust in Jesus? If you are a Christian, how did it come about?

_____

_____

_____

_____

Questions for your mom to ask you:

How do you think it must have felt for God to give His One and Only Son to die for us?

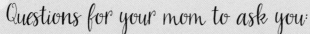

_____

_____

_____

_____

_____

What do you think it means to believe in Jesus?

_____

_____

_____

_____

_____

This Week

Look up John 3:16 and write it down. Or put it on your phone and try to memorize it. If it's important enough for people to put on a sign for all to see, it's worth memorizing!

Keep Going

Find some time this week and look up the types of religions below on the Internet (only with Mom's help!). Draw a line to match the major religions with their beliefs about God.

Hinduism This religion believes in many different gods and goddesses.

New Age This religion believes in one supreme God who desires to have a relationship with them. He is loving and compassionate.

Christianity This religion believes there is no God at all.

Buddhism This religion believes in one supreme God (Allah), but they are unable to have a relationship with him. He is strict and powerful.

Islam This religion believes they are God.

Week 49:
Say It Like You Mean It

Bible Reading

Godly sorrow brings repentance that leads to salvation and leaves no regret, but worldly sorrow brings death.
—2 Corinthians 7:10 NIV

Read the passage aloud and listen carefully for the answers to the following questions:

What kind of sorrow brings repentance (a change in our thoughts and behavior)?

_____

What kind of sorrow brings death?

_____

Bringing It Home

For the second time in one week, Caroline sat in her room. She had been sent there by her parents to "think about what she had done wrong." This time, she was in trouble for being disrespectful to her mother when she reminded Caroline to do the dishes. Her parents had had several talks with her about her bad attitude lately, and deep down Caroline knew they were right. She was in a bad habit of using the wrong tone of voice with her mother, but she felt like her mother was always getting on to her about something. When her mother reminded her to do the dishes, she was busy watching her favorite show. Instead of pausing the show and getting the dishes done, she grumbled and said, "I'm busy, Mom. It's not like the dirty dishes are going anywhere. They'll still be there after my show."

Caroline's dad happened to walk into the room and heard her. Everything went downhill from there. "Caroline, I don't like your tone. You are to respect your mother!" After that he demanded she do the dishes right away and apologize to her mom. "Fine, I'm sorry!" Caroline huffed as she turned off her show and stomped into the kitchen. She was so frustrated that she made sure to bang and clatter the pots and pans as loudly as possible while she washed them. Of course, that only made her dad even more mad. "Caroline, you are clearly not sorry. Your attitude is still disrespectful. After the dishes, you can go to your room and think about it. And you can do the dishes for the remainder of this week, as well."

As Caroline sat in her room, she knew her dad was right and she owed her parents an apology for the way she had been treating them lately. Deep down, she hated when they were disappointed in her. Most of all, she hated to disappoint God. Maybe a good start was to apologize to God first and then talk to her parents.

What does God's Word say?

In 2 Corinthians 7:10, the apostle Paul talked about two types of sorrow. There is a godly sorrow, which is a sincere sorrow over the impact our sin has on our relationship with God. Godly sorrow respects how He paid a very high price for our sin (His Son's death on the cross). If we have a godly sorrow, we mourn (feel sadness) because we have grieved the heart of God (and possibly others). This type of sorrow usually leads to repentance. If you look up the word *repentance*, you will find words like *regret* or *remorse*.

The biblical meaning of the word *repentance*, goes a bit deeper and means "a change of mind." In other words, the person who has a godly sorrow over a sin is less likely to repeat the sin again because she feels regret over how it impacted her relationship with God. She experiences "a change of mind" over the sin and desire to do the right thing. This type of sorrow leads to salvation, because in order to become a Christian, we must be truly sorry for our sins and recognize that Jesus paid the price for them. Believing in Jesus leads to salvation (life after death).

On the other hand, worldly sorrow is not genuine or sincere. If there is grief or remorse, it is usually because the person got caught or felt obligated to apologize for the sin. The person will most likely repeat the sin again because they haven't had "a change of mind" over the sin. This type of sorrow can lead to death if a person goes their entire life without expressing sorrow over their sin. To avoid eternal death, they must turn to Jesus (repent) and accept His offer of forgiveness.

Think About It

Have you ever said you are sorry for something without really meaning it?

Talk About It

Questions to ask your mom:

Can you think of a time when you displayed "worldly sorrow" because you were caught, but you weren't truly sorry? What was it?

_____

_____

_____

_____

Why is "godly sorrow" important if we want to change our attitude or behavior?

_____

_____

_____

_____

Questions for your mom to ask you:

Is it difficult for you to apologize (on your own) when you've done something wrong, or do you usually only apologize if you're told to?

If yes, why is apologizing difficult for you?

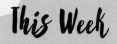

This Week

Keep a record of all the times you hear someone (yourself included!) say they are sorry for something this week. Write down the apologies in your journal, and if they sounded like examples of "godly sorrow" or worldly sorrow."

Keep Going

Read the examples of apologies below and determine if it is a godly sorrow or a worldly sorrow. Circle your choice.

1. Alyssa borrows her sister's shirt without asking. Her mother tells her she needs to return the shirt and apologize. Alyssa changes her shirt and walks by her sister's room, throws the shirt into the doorway, and mumbles, "I'm sorry I took your stupid shirt."

    Godly sorrow   Worldly sorrow

2. Samantha was supposed to save a seat at lunch for one of her friends, but she gets busy talking and forgets. When her friend walks up, all the seats are taken. The friend looks over at Samantha, rolls her eyes, and keeps on walking. Samantha yells after her, "Sorrrrrry! I'm not perfect, ya know?!"

    Godly sorrow   Worldly sorrow

3. Amanda said something rude to one of her friends and heard from someone else that it had hurt her friend's feelings. Amanda calls her after school and tells her, "I am so sorry for hurting your feelings. That is not really who I am, and I hope you can forgive me."

Godly sorrow　　　　　　Worldly sorrow

4. Tessa races past her sister and shoves her out of the way so she can get to the front passenger seat first. Her sister tells her mom when she gets to the car, and Tessa's mom makes her apologize to her sister. As punishment, Tessa has to sit in the backseat. Tessa says to her sister, "Sorry I shoved you, tattletale."

Godly sorrow　　　　　　Worldly sorrow

5. Rachel was playing a game on her tablet before bedtime and forgot to get her backpack ready for school the next morning. When she gets to school, she realizes she left her homework at home on her desk. She calls her mom and says, "Mom, I am so sorry, but I forgot to pack my backpack last night and left my homework at home. Can you please bring it to me? I'll try to be more responsible next time."

Godly sorrow　　　　　　Worldly sorrow

Week 50:
More Fruit, Please

Bible Reading

But the fruit of the Spirit is love, joy, peace, patience, kindness, goodness, faith, gentleness, self-control. Against such things there is no law.
—Galatians 5:22-23

Read the passage aloud and listen carefully for the answers to the following questions:

What are some of the fruits of the Spirit?

What does the verse mean by the word Spirit?

Bringing It Home

Sadie knew the minute she walked into her bedroom that her little sister had been there. There were shirts hanging out of her dresser drawers, and her closet doors were left open. Sadie was a neat freak and always kept her room tidy. Her sister, on the other hand, was a slob—and worst of all, a clothes thief! They were two years apart in age, but wore the same size clothes—which Sadie hated. To make matters worse, they also wore the same size shoe. As Sadie looked around her room, her blood began to boil when she saw her tablet on her desk. Her sister had taken a selfie and saved the picture as Sadie's screensaver. Ugh, not funny. How much longer until she graduated and moved away to college?! She wasn't sure she could survive eight more years of living with an annoying little sister.

Before she left her room to track down her sister to let her have it, she paused and remembered that she was supposed to be different now. A few months before, she had given her life to Christ at summer camp, and she was working hard to become more like Jesus. She knew Jesus

probably wouldn't clobber someone for borrowing His shirt. In fact, she remembered a verse in the Bible where He said if anyone takes away your coat, you should offer them your shirt as well. But then again, Jesus had never met Sadie's sister!

Before leaving her room, Sadie decided to pray and ask Jesus to help her respond with patience and gentleness. On her own, she knew it wasn't possible to contain her temper, but with Jesus' help, her sister just might live another day!

What does God's Word say?

When someone becomes a Christian (believes Jesus died for her sins), the Holy Spirit comes to live in her heart. God is present in three forms: the Father, the Son, and the Holy Spirit. In John 14:26, Jesus calls the Holy Spirit "the Helper" (ESV) who has been sent by the Father in the name of Jesus. The Holy Spirit will guide us and help us remember the teachings of Christ. As we seek to be more like Jesus, we will display (show off) the "fruits of the Spirit" (evidence or proof that we are believers, and that the Holy Spirit lives in our hearts).

Jesus possessed all of the fruits of the Spirit. Christians are not perfect, but as they grow in their relationship with Christ, they should look different than the rest of the world. For example, if they are tempted to be unkind or unloving, the Spirit, or Christ living within them, will remind them to be more like Him. This is one way others know we are different. Others should be drawn to those who are Christians because of the fruits of the Spirit that are visible in their lives.

Think About It

If you have accepted Christ
(you believe He died for your sins),
did you know the Holy Spirit came
to live in your heart?

Talk About It

Questions to ask your mom:

Which of the fruits of the Spirit would others say you possess?

_____

_____

_____

_____

_____

Which ones are struggles for you?

_____

_____

_____

_____

_____

Questions for your mom to ask you:

Which of the fruits of the Spirit would others say you possess?

_____

_____

_____

_____

_____

Which ones are struggles for you?

_____

_____

_____

_____

This Week

Write down the nine fruits of the Spirit on a blank page in your journal or notebook. Leave plenty of space between each one. Each day look at the list to see if you demonstrated any of the fruits of the Spirit during that day. If so, write them down and how you displayed each one. At the end of the week, check back over your list to see how many of the fruits of the Spirit you demonstrated in one week. Have your mom do the same thing so you can compare lists next week.

Keep Going

Can you find all the fruits of the Spirit in the puzzle below?

```
S  A  S  U  L  G  E  F  U  K  F  S  H  A  B
W  E  B  O  C  Y  R  O  W  K  S  D  T  X  X
Q  W  L  S  R  X  R  X  P  E  U  F  I  T  A
D  U  R  F  O  T  F  O  N  S  B  B  A  A  S
I  B  C  L  C  L  W  E  D  S  Z  E  F  B  X
A  P  D  D  B  O  L  U  S  N  E  Q  C  S  M
C  P  E  L  N  T  N  E  E  V  O  L  L  O  Z
C  M  K  A  N  Q  N  T  V  Q  C  M  X  S  E
N  Z  C  E  C  D  P  W  R  I  C  K  E  M  S
V  O  G  R  N  E  J  O  Y  O  H  Q  N  A  Z
S  E  P  I  V  W  X  X  O  Z  L  A  Q  M  E
T  O  K  O  P  Q  T  X  D  W  B  G  K  E  U
B  H  S  S  E  N  D  O  O  G  Y  Q  L  J  D
Z  T  E  C  N  E  I  T  A  P  T  F  E  B  G
Q  L  D  Q  X  R  P  E  Y  S  E  P  O  U  O
```

love	patience	faith
joy	kindness	gentleness
peace	goodness	self-control

Week 51:
Do You Have a Reservation?

Bible Reading

In My Father's house are many dwelling places; if not, I would have told you. I am going away to prepare a place for you. If I go away and prepare a place for you, I will come back and receive you to Myself, so that where I am you may be also.
— John 14:2–3

Read the passage aloud and listen carefully for the answers to the following questions:

What did Jesus say was in His Father's house?

_____

_____

What did He say He was going away to prepare?

_____

_____

Bringing It Home

Heaven. Angels. Clouds. Harps. It was midnight, and Cora's friends at the sleepover started talking about heaven and what they thought it might be like. Everyone seemed to have their own ideas when it came to heaven. One of the girls talked about how she was looking forward to seeing her grandpa who had gone to be with Jesus a few years before. She said the pastor of her grandpa's church talked about a Bible verse at the funeral that said Jesus had prepared a place in heaven for believers. Cora didn't go to church and hadn't read much of the Bible, so she didn't know what to think. What about the people who didn't believe in Jesus? She thought everyone got to go to heaven—unless you were a really horrible person or something.

And where is this heaven place? She always assumed it was somewhere up above the clouds, but she sure hoped it had a floor! And books to read. And movies to watch. And lots of snacks. And her very own tablet so she didn't have to share! After her friends had dozed off, she lay awake wondering about this heaven place. Maybe she would talk to

her mom about it when she got home. Maybe they could start going to church again. They used to go when she was little, and she wasn't sure why they had stopped going. The older she got, the more curious she was becoming about God. Church seemed like a good place to go to get answers to her questions about God and heaven.

What does God's Word say?

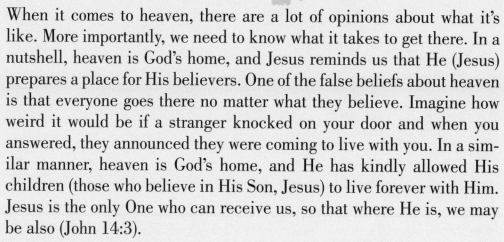

When it comes to heaven, there are a lot of opinions about what it's like. More importantly, we need to know what it takes to get there. In a nutshell, heaven is God's home, and Jesus reminds us that He (Jesus) prepares a place for His believers. One of the false beliefs about heaven is that everyone goes there no matter what they believe. Imagine how weird it would be if a stranger knocked on your door and when you answered, they announced they were coming to live with you. In a similar manner, heaven is God's home, and He has kindly allowed His children (those who believe in His Son, Jesus) to live forever with Him. Jesus is the only One who can receive us, so that where He is, we may be also (John 14:3).

For those who are believers, there is no need to feel anxious or worried about heaven. In fact, right before Jesus talked about preparing a place for believers, He said, "Your heart must not be troubled. Believe in God; believe also in Me" (John 14:1). As we grow in our relationship with Christ, we will look forward to a day when we can live together for all eternity in God's house.

Think About It

Have you thought much about heaven and what it is like?

Talk About It

Questions to ask your mom:

When you were my age, did you think about heaven much? If yes, what did you imagine it was like?

Does it bring you comfort to know that Jesus has prepared a place for His believers?

_____

Questions for your mom to ask you:

Does it make you feel uneasy to talk about heaven? Why or why not?

_____

_____

_____

_____

_____

_____

Does it bring you comfort to know that Jesus has prepared a place for His believers?

_____

This Week

Draw a picture in the space below of what you think heaven looks like.

Keep Going

There are many myths about heaven that the Bible doesn't support. Look up the verses below to determine if the statements about eternity and heaven are true or false. Circle your choice.

1. It is easy to get into heaven (Matthew 7:13–14).

    True   False

2. Jesus promises believers He will return and take them to heaven (John 14:2–3).

    True   False

3. We will still feel sadness and pain at times in heaven (Revelation 21:4).

    True   False

4. In heaven, there will be no more night (Revelation 22:5).

    True   False

5. If you are married on earth, you will still be married in heaven (Matthew 22:30).

   True   False

6. God created the heavens (Isaiah 48:13).

   True   False

7. In heaven, we won't have the same bodies we have now (2 Corinthians 5:1).

   True   False

Week 52:
Who Do You Say I Am?

Bible Reading

He asked them, "who do you say that I am?" Simon Peter answered, "You are the Messiah, the Son of the living God!"
—Matthew 16:15-16

Read the passage aloud and listen carefully for the answers to the following questions:

What question did Jesus ask His disciples?

_____

_____

What was Simon Peter's answer?

_____

_____

_____

Bringing It Home

Emory stared in disbelief at the B+ written on top of her social studies test on world religions. She was used to getting all A's, so a B+ came as a shocker. She had studied hard and felt well prepared for the test. What had happened? She began to look over the questions to see what her teacher had marked wrong. Everything looked good on the multiple-choice questions and the fill-in-the-blanks. She turned the test over, and that's when she saw a big red *x* beside one of the short essay questions. The instructions had said to give a brief description of Buddha, Mohammad, and Jesus and describe their key differences. Her teacher had highlighted part of her answer where she stated that Jesus was the Son of God and the only way to the one true God. Beside the question, her teacher had written a note saying, "I wouldn't have counted it wrong if you had said that Jesus 'claimed' to be the Son of God and the only way to God, but you cannot state it as a fact."

Emory's heart sank. *But I can state it as a fact because I believe with all my heart that it is a fact*, she thought. The instructions had said to describe the three key religious figures and point out their differences. She had followed the instructions. Buddha and Mohammad never claimed to be God. But Jesus did. *How could my answer be wrong?* she wondered. Most everyone agreed that Jesus was a good person, but how could He be a good person if He was telling a lie when He said He was the Son of God? She knew that not everyone was going to believe in Jesus, and she respected that; but she wanted the same respect. Maybe she would talk to her teacher about it after school. She knew she had honored God with her answer and prayed He would give her the words to say.

What does God's Word say?

Your answer to Jesus' question, "Who do you say that I am?" may be the most important question you will ever have to consider in your lifetime. Becoming a Christian rests upon believing that Jesus is the Messiah, the Son of the living God. *Messiah* means "the promised and expected deliverer." The birth, death, and resurrection (when Jesus rose from the dead) was foretold in the Bible long before Jesus was even born. Jesus came to deliver us from our sins and pay the price so that we could have a relationship with God. He is the expected deliverer and the only One who can bridge the gap between man and God.

Maybe you've heard the term *saved* when someone is talking about becoming a Christian. If someone is saved from their sins, it means they believe that Jesus paid the penalty for their sin and saved them from the consequences of sin (death or separation from God). We all die, but those who believe in Jesus will live forever and experience life after death (in heaven) with God. You cannot be saved without believing Jesus is the Messiah, the Son of the living God. You cannot be saved by believing Jesus was just a good man, or a good teacher, or even a prophet (like Mohammad of the Islam faith). So, let me ask you a question: Who do you say He is?

Think About It

Do you think the question Jesus asked His disciples was an important one for every person to consider?

Talk About It

Questions to ask your mom:

Have you ever had a conversation with someone who didn't believe Jesus is the Son of God? How did you respond?

If He asked you the question, "Who do you say that I am?" how would you answer?

_____

_____

_____

_____

_____

_____

_____

Questions for your mom to ask you:

Why do you think some people don't believe Jesus was the Son of God?

_____

_____

_____

_____

_____

If He asked you the question, "Who do you say that I am?" what would you say?

_____

_____

_____

_____

_____

_____

This Week

Take some time to think seriously about your answer to the question Jesus asked His disciples: "Who do you say that I am?" Write a letter to Jesus in your journal and include your answer to the question.

Keep Going

Who is Jesus?

Complete the crossword puzzle below. Look up the Bible verses if you need a clue.

Across

3. At the name of Jesus, every _____ will bow. (Philippians 2:10)

5. Jesus Christ is the same yesterday, today, and _____. (Hebrews 13:8)

7. Jesus asked God to _____ those who divided up His clothing while He was dying on the cross. (Luke 23:34)

8. Jesus did not commit ____. (1 Peter 2:21–22)

9. All _____ has been given to Jesus. (Matthew 28:18)

10. All things have been _____ through Jesus and for Jesus. (Colossians 1:16)

Down

1. Jesus came to seek and to _____ those who were lost. (Luke 19:10)

2. Every _____ will confess that Jesus Christ is Lord. (Philippians 2:11)

4. The angels _____ Jesus. (Hebrews 1:6)

6. Jesus humbled Himself by becoming _____ to the point of death. (Philippians 2:8)

How to Become a Christian

Becoming a Christian is the most important decision you will ever make in your life. Read each step below very carefully to make sure you understand what each one means.

We learn about God's love in the Bible.

For God loved the world in this way: He gave his One and Only Son, so that everyone who believes in Him will not perish but have eternal life.—John 3:16

Perish means to die and to be apart from God—forever. God loves you so much and wants you to have *eternal life* in heaven where you are with Him forever.

If you understand what John 3:16 means, put a check here:_____

All of us have sinned.

For all have sinned and fall short of the glory of God. —Romans 3:23

You may have heard someone say, "I'm only human—nobody's perfect." This Bible verse says the same thing: We are all sinners. No one is perfect. When we sin, we do things that are wrong—things that God would not agree with. The verse says we fall short of "God's glorious standard." In order to meet God's standard, we would have to be perfect and stay that way . . . forever. Obviously, that's impossible since we are

born sinners and we will continue to sin. But before you start to worry that you don't meet His standard, just wait. There's good news ahead.

If you understand what John 3:16 means, put a check here:_____

Sin has a penalty (punishment).

For the wages [cost] of sin is death.—Romans 6:23

Our punishment is separation from God's blessings, favor, and love. When we die, we will receive God's wrath for all eternity unless payment is made for sin. The Bible teaches that those who choose to reject God will spend eternity in a place called hell. You may have heard some bad things about hell, but the worst part about hell is that you are in a place where you are punished forever.

If you understand what John 3:16 means, put a check here:_____

Christ has paid the price for our sins!

But God proves His own love for us in that while we were still sinners, Christ died for us!—Romans 5:8

The Bible teaches that Jesus Christ is the perfect Son of God. He never sinned, and He has paid the price for all your sins. The Bible says that Christ loved you enough to die for you. Pretty amazing!

If you understand what John 3:16 means, put a check here:_____

Salvation (life in heaven) is a free gift.

For you are saved by grace through faith, and this is not from yourselves; it is God's gift—not from works, so that no one can boast.—Ephesians 2:8–9

The word *grace* means "a gift we don't deserve." That gift is forgiveness from your sins and eternal life. God's gift to you is free. You do not have to work for a gift. That's why it's called a gift. All you have to do is receive it. Believe with all your heart that Jesus Christ died for you and paid the price for your sins!

If you understand what John 3:16 means, put a check here:_____

You must receive Him.

But to all who did receive Him, He gave them the right to be children of God.—John 1:12

Christ has died for your sins so you can be forgiven. However, you must choose to believe in Him and give Him control of your life. When you receive Christ into your heart, you become a child of God. The Christian life is a personal relationship with God through Jesus Christ. Just like you have a relationship with a best friend, you can have a relationship with God through Jesus. He never takes His of salvation gift back, so you don't have to worry about losing it. It is yours forever.

If you understand what John 3:16 means, put a check here:_____

So, what do you think about God's offer of forgiveness? Is this a gift you want to accept? If so, tell God. You don't have to say a fancy prayer—just talk to Him and tell Him that you believe that Jesus died on the cross for your sins and you want Him to save you. That's all it takes! Stop and say a prayer right now.

Did you say a prayer and accept God's gift of forgiveness? _____

If you answered yes, congratulations! You are a Christian! If you aren't quite sure if you are ready to accept God's gift of forgiveness, talk to someone who can help—your pastor, parents, or a relative. Tell them you want to know more about being a Christian!

(Adapted from "Your Christian Life," Billy Graham Evangelistic Association, 1997)